A Hole in My Soul
❧ *my father's sin* ❧

May God be the One who fills the hole in your Soul! Blessing Java

Java L. Collins

Pulished by JimSam Inc.
P. O.. Box 3363
Riverview, FL 33568
www.JimSamInc.com

Scripture quotations are taken from the
King James Version of the Holy Bible.

Library of Congress Cataloging-in-Publication Data

Collins, Java L.
  A hole in my soul : my father's sin / Java L. Collins.
    p. cm.
  Includes bibliographical references.
  ISBN-13: 978-0-9820587-7-0 (pbk.)
  ISBN-10: 0-9820587-7-2 (pbk.)
  1. Fatherhood. 2. Fathers--United States. 3. African American
fathers. 4. Father and child--United States. I. Title.
  HQ756.C628 2009
  248.8'421--dc22

                                        2009017104

Cover Design:
Kate Goodberry
Goodberry Design Company
506 West Harvey Street
Philadelphia, PA 19144
www.goodberrydesign.com

Dedication

To God, my Heavenly Father, whom I love more than life itself; to my natural father, Elmore Wiley, Jr., I love you, thank you for your desire to dream; and to my spiritual father, Dr. Stephen Rathod, I thank God for the gift of fathering in you and thank you for showing me how to be a daughter. There were several others who so graciously helped me, but I felt it more appropriate to acknowledge at this time those mentioned here. I do not take the work of the others lightly. I love them and pray continually for God to bless them.

However, there is one person I wish to honor by giving credit where credit is due: to my mother, Norma J. Collins-Anderson. Family meant a lot to my mother and was first in her life. There were times she sacrificed and went without so my five sisters and I could have. It was her message of love, forgiveness and togetherness which she tried to send to help us believe in ourselves, in what we could and could not do. She encouraged us, disciplined us and provided for us, but most of all, she loved us with every breath in her body. We were able to see her strengths, her weaknesses and realize those were part of the essence of her being, and it never negated her love for us. With eternal admiration to her memory, I praise God for her.

I love stories of journeys, of dreams, of hopes, of triumphs, especially about women who have overcome. I love stories that give me wisdom, guidance, hope, courage and laughter. You might be hesitant as you launch on this journey and I do not blame you; so was I. I can only tell you that I understand; though painful and confronting, my hope has opened a whole new life for me.

So whether you are asking questions, seeking answers or are in the process of transforming yourself, my prayer is that this book will serve as a tool and be a companion to you. I desire for it to provide markers, insights, questions, yet motivate you, inspire you and bless you. I pray that its boldness and meaning empower you to step out of the shadow of being a bastard and dare to dream, to change, to be. May God be with you on this crossing.

Java L. Collins

Foreword

As a natural father of three and spiritual father of many, it is only fitting that a father should say a word for his spiritual daughter. Too often as fathers we curse our children. It hurts and damages their self-esteem and their worth. A father is called to bless, provide and train his children for the Lord. On Father's Day, I watched my spiritual daughter finally become free of the traps that occur when a father curses his child.

Throughout Bible history, fathers were to bless their children, but on many occasions this was not so. An example is with Jacob and his sons. In Genesis, the 49th chapter, Jacob begins to pronounce blessings and curses on each of his children, and in each case gives the reason why. Jacob cursed Simeon and Levi when they took it upon themselves to avenge their sister's rape and he accused them of cursing his name and bringing him shame. In Genesis, the 34th chapter tells of the incident and how this father did nothing to protect or avenge this terrible thing that had happened to his daughter, but these two brothers devised a scheme and carried it out to avenge their sister.

Being cursed by your father is a terrible thing! It brings forth feelings of not being loved, feelings of rejection and abandonment. Fathers can destroy you emotionally and then, in turn, you end up destroying your children. There is power in the words of your mouth as a father. Your words can form or deform your child's life.

Nevertheless as my spiritual daughter experienced that Sunday, a curse can be broken! Exodus the 32nd chapter, verses seven through thirty-five, show this. Remember Jacob cursed Levi. Levi represents the tribe of Levites, who were the priests. In a brief overview, when Moses went to the mountaintop to receive the Ten Commandments, God told him to go back down because the people were sinning against Him. Upon Moses' return in verse twenty-six, he says, *"Who is on the Lord's side? Let him come unto me. And all the sons of Levi gathered themselves together unto him."* Further down in verse twenty-nine Moses says, *"Consecrate yourselves today to the Lord, even every man upon his son, and upon his brother; that he may bestow upon you a blessing this day."* Instead of the Levites being cursed as they previously were by their natural father, their heavenly Father now blessed them.

The curse has been broken because my spiritual daughter, like the Levites, has chosen to obey God. God is on her side and He can be on your side too. As you read this book, open your heart and let God fill the hole left in your soul by the curses of your fathers or any other person who has spoken words which have taken you into bondage, into captivity. Know this, there is no curse stronger than God! Blessings to you as you journey forth.

Dr. Stephen Rathod
Senior Pastor
Covenant Family Church

To Uncle J

Hey Now!

Love, J

Contents

❧ A Letter to My Father ❧

" . . . shall I give my firstborn for
my transgression, the fruit of my body
for the sin of my soul?
~ Micah 6:7b

It is a wise father
who knows his own child.
~ Shakespeare

Dearest Dad,

It is not my desire to write this book to cause you pain or show you in any unfavorable light. I am writing this to free myself, as well as others who are like me. Please understand I am grateful for the things you have done for me, even though at times it appeared to me to be an afterthought.

For a while, your distance made me see myself only as the by-product of my parents' sin, but now like the Virginia Slim commercial says, "I've come a long way, baby!" It took some time working through the pain, hurt, wounds and heartaches to no longer see myself as a bastard, a byproduct of sin; however, God is faithful.

I look at you and see the part of me that dreams, forever wanting to escape the shadows and demands of others. Though my mother taught me how to survive, you showed me how to view every conversation with you as a learning experience. Our conversations provided pieces to the puzzle I needed to help in making me whole. Your words helped me realize I have choices available to me and that I no longer have to think about the what-ifs; all I need is to "just do it!" Your insight has been very helpful.

I am choosing to let my past teach me now and I am choosing to make a change for the future generations which will come after me. I am choosing to break – no destroy – the cycle to keep it from repeating itself.

I will forever love you!

Your Eldest Daughter,
Java L. Collins

❧ Introduction ❦

"Other things may change us,
but we start and end with family."
~ Unknown

When we go from one extreme to another we have no balance. I wanted balance in my life but before I could have balance, I had to recognize the imbalance for what it was and take yet another journey into my life for fulfillment. I pursued the spiritual with a passion and now I had to pursue the natural just the same – go to depths and look at meanings I would not have glanced at before. Some places in my journey did not want to be removed or uprooted because of the pain, and some easily came loose because of previous prodding. My thoughts, memories and feelings are mine and mine alone. At no time do I try to explain or interject how or what someone else is feeling. My only goal was I wanted to be free.

This project came about as I began a journey to discover myself. It was an adventure to continue to explore the many facets that make up my being. I had the feeling something was missing in my life and could not quite put my finger on it.

During a road trip with my son, we were having a conversation in which I asked a question that had been lingering in the back of my mind. Did he feel he had a good childhood? His reply stunned me somewhat. It was *"You mean besides me having to quote Bible verses and getting into trouble for some things that I did not do?"* I smiled and said, *"Yes, in spite of those things."* Then he turned to me and with the sincerest eyes spoke, *"I wish I had had a father in the home."*

His answer genuinely surprised me because like most single parents I had to fulfill the role of both mother and father after my divorce. His sincerity made me determined to confront my own issues, my own desire, my own wish that my natural father – not a stepfather or the so-called uncles – had been in the home. My mother's brother, Uncle Warren (aka Uncle J), became father and mentor to both my eldest sister and me. He opened a whole new avenue of life to us, but still I wanted a father. I wanted the same thing my son was echoing to me.

Memories flooded my mind that even as a young girl I often wondered *what I did to make my father not want me,* especially when I discovered he was less than six hours away from me and living with his family – a wife, three daughters and a son. What did I do? Why did he not own up to me? Why did he not love me enough to be a part of raising me? Did he want to know who I was or be a part in developing who I was to become?

I admit I was curious and wanted to know who this man was who so fascinated my mother that she conceived a child with him. While at the same time, I was puzzled that he could leave as if the creation of this child had never occurred. It was not until I had a disturbing dream that I finally got the courage to ask my mother before her death about my father. My mother was a fair woman and she never said anything but good things about my father, which further enforced the *"it-must-be-me"* syndrome. If my mother had anything bad to say about my father, then she carried that information with her to her grave.

Further reflection into my life led me to a startling realization! By my father not being a part of my life, he had left me with fragments and a denied inheritance. I did not know what a *"bastard"* was until I heard it used by an aunt one day and being the brilliant child I am (smile), I went to the dictionary and by sounding it out, looked up the word.

> *Bastard: an illegitimate child; inferior; illegitimate in birth; counterfeit.*

Confused by the word "illegitimate," I proceeded to look it up and found:

> *Illegitimate: not legitimate; unlawful; born out of wedlock*

These words surely could not be describing me. I ran to my mother and asked her "Am I a bastard?" and she asked where had I heard that from and I informed her the dictionary. In the best way she could, she tried to console me and make the words I just read seem like nothing major, but in my heart I knew it was.

Being a bastard child, I felt I could not put any claim on an inheritance, naturally or spiritually. I began to focus on how not knowing my rights as a daughter ran parallel to my rights as a spiritual daughter, God's daughter, but also how not having a father to impart to me and impact my life had left a hole in my soul, in the depth of my being. A question I had kept asking myself was *"Why is the spirit of rejection so deep in me?"* I learned when someone I care for or love denied me in any way, I took it personally, even though it was not. This damaged my psyche, my being; it caused the hole in me to deepen, leaving me confused about who I was.

I mentioned the words *"fatherhood fragments."* I heard this term used during one of my graduate courses. What I mean when I say this is in reference to the sleepover boyfriends, ex-boyfriends, uncles, grandfathers (usually maternal), and sometimes, yet very seldom, the men in the church. I was blessed to go to a church where the senior pastor, assistant pastor and youth pastor took time with my son, even though they could not replace or fill the void of his father. They were positive images or role models that greatly impacted his life. Being African-American, one would venture to think that because of the role of slavery, many African-American men do not quite grasp the role of fatherhood and play out the hand society expects of them – one of rejection and abandonment.

When a father is not in the home, or if he is in the home and not available, the child will never experience the love of a father firsthand, but more so as an onlooker, a spectator. The right to claim a wholesome relationship with the father has become *"access denied."* The sad part is both parties miss out on a wonderful chance to build and have a lasting, worthwhile relationship.

I love to read, research and explore. When I read novels like *Silas Marner* by George Eliot or *Wuthering Heights* by Emily Brontë, I began to wonder what went wrong on my end. These books focused on the paternal love, devotion and commitment of a father while looking at the neglect and abuse as well. Sometimes we all read the fairy tales and wish our lives were like that because we know how the story ends – they lived happily ever after, but again those are just books and the stories do end. The story of life does not end until death and even then, what one has done lives on in the stories told and retold by loved ones.

During my quest I noticed there were many studies dealing with being fatherless, father-daughter, father-son, but none quite addressed the subject I was looking into – the bastard or the illegitimate child and how that child was affected naturally and spiritually. The studies I looked at tried to say *why or how* men viewed fatherhood. Is it a problem? Yes. Are families expendable? No. Do children not play into the fathers' plans? They should, they helped create them. Is there a need for fathers? Absolutely. Do we believe in the idea of fatherhood anymore? Now that one is questionable.

In the book of Genesis, it displays one of the most prominent pictures of fatherhood. Abraham (Abram) at the insistence of Sarah (Sarai) had produced a child from Sarah's handmaiden, Hagar, which brought forth Ishmael. Though he was an illegitimate son by all rights, Ishmael would not be denied by his father nor forgotten by God. Knowing he could have turned his back on Ishmael, Abraham helped rear Ishmael until the time came for Ishmael and his mother, Hagar, to leave, but even then God promised Abraham He would make a nation out of Ishmael. So in both aspects Ishmael received both his natural and spiritual inheritance, and if it can happen for him, why can it not happen for me? Abraham's role in Ishmael's life showed that when a father plays an active role in the life of his child or children, what comes of it is the production of a worthwhile adult, not one who just knows how to survive.

After reading Genesis and reviewing the studies on fatherhood, these things plagued my mind and made me more determined to conquer the monster that had undermined my beliefs, my security, my protection, my rights and my inheritance, both naturally and spiritually. If you are interested in addressing the hole in your soul, then join me as I explore some avenues to find a way to bring healing to my soul and to claiming my inheritance to live in what is rightfully mine.

I believe this book will help both males and females, though written from my own personal experiences. This book was written for all to read and to respond to. Also, though I do not address it, it is my prayer those who have lost their fathers – through death as a young or older child – may be healed by some parts of this book and put on a path to being made whole.

Let me say here that if your father died, there is probably no difference in how you feel. It is almost the same as having a father leave or having no father at all; the results are the same. It hurts, leaving you with a hole all the same. With death, you grieve over what you have lost, but you still feel rejected, abandoned and unloved – still trying to figure out how you can make it right. You are left to struggle with the hole and having everyone tell you it is all right, for it was God's will. My prayer is that as you read this book your hole will begin to be filled. Through this journey I have learned to thank God I am **not** someone else and I am on my way to being only who I am, raised and groomed by the Father for His use.

Chapter 1
❧ A Fatherless Generation ❧

"The family was ordained of God
that children might be trained up for Him . . ."
~ Pope Leo XII (1810-1903)

I have come to realize all fathers have a story to tell – whether it is trying to get us to sympathize with the plight of a teenage father, a deadbeat dad, a child molester, or even hearing clearly their reasons for not being there. They all have a story to tell. Regardless, a father's absence in the home does have a major effect upon a child's upbringing. Society views a father leaving his responsibilities as damaging, but it is something a person has to get used to. Figuratively, the leaving or absent father represents fatherhood dying in the eyes of the child and death is usually final.

Fatherhood in America contains two faces – one that appears to be concerned and affectionate, and the other which appears to be tense and authoritarian. In Greek the word for father is *pater*, which stands for protector. As the absence of a father becomes a more routine, commonplace fixture in the lives of his children, as time goes by the pain becomes a dull ache, never disappearing, yet always present. It is a void the child tries desperately to fill but never can. Who cries for the bastard? Do men even think about the mark that is left when they choose (whether you left on your own or were asked to leave, you still made a choice) to walk out of a child's life?

One of the main excuses I have heard is that "*it was the best that your mama could do while raising you.*" Maybe this is because it has been a widely held belief that women were considered to be the more moral of the two parents. This is the reason why the responsibility of childrearing was delegated to her, even in civilizations where culture and tradition supported a patriarchal society. The sad part is that men have greatly relinquished their participation in childrearing, even in disciplining, in exchange for being able to come home and find it nice, clean and peaceful. Many men who do stay in the home view their role as only one thing – being the breadwinner, the provider, and nothing more. However, with the majority of heads of households being women, a belief has now come to light that the majority of men could not pull off the role of both mother and father to the extent women have done, or certainly not quite as effectively.

With the social atmosphere continually evolving, imagine if my generation were *"at-risk,"* how much more so is today's generation? As the new generation comes forth, should we be surprised that with the lack of a father being present, they have no remorse, conscious or comprehension? They move around like a person unable to tell right from wrong, good from evil.

In this day and age if you want to read some pretty scary figures, look at these 2003 statistics, gathered from the United States Census Bureau:

- Fatherless homes account for 63% of youth suicide;
- Fatherless homes account for 90% of homeless/runaway children;
- Fatherless homes account for 85% of children with behavior problems;
- Fatherless homes account for 71% of high school dropouts;
- Fatherless homes account for 85% of youths in prison, well over 50% of teen mothers;

- 40% of children in America live in homes with no fathers;
- 50% of children in America will have very limited contact with their fathers before the age of 18 for the majority, the natural father did not live in the home;
- On most birth certificates, two out of three never legally identify the father;
- More than one-third of all childbirths occur outside of the marriage.

Though not published, it is believed a certain percentage of fathers voluntarily abandon, reject or deny their children, their own flesh and blood. And note that poverty is on the rise with studies showing fatherlessness, whether the father is unemployed, underemployed or not there in the home, to be a contributing factor.

Society used to believe the father's role was of lesser importance in childrearing than the mother's; however, **now** the Bible and society have agreed on something. They both believe a father's role should be to endow or impart, provide, protect, be a caregiver and help in forming a child's behavior. A father's role is viewed as being potentially important and a significant part of the process in family life.

David Blankenhorn, author of *Fatherless America: Confronting Our Most Urgent Social Problem*, made two important statements in his book. The first was that (paraphrased) "because of this fatherlessness it is likely to change the shape of our society ... America will be divided by the fault line of patrimony." He shows we constantly complain about rising crime, guns, teen pregnancies, but yet we remain silent about the child who has no father, whether it was intentional or not.

The other point he made was "Today's story of fatherhood features one dimensional characters, an unbelievable plot and an unhappy ending . . . (however) a good society celebrates the ideal of the man who puts his family first." In this time period, who defines fatherhood and its expectations? I agree with Mr. Blankenhorn when he says fatherlessness is the leading cause of the declining of a child's well-being in our society.

The majority of mothers have always gone out on a limb to provide, some even working two or three jobs just to make ends meet. Too often what evolves now are young (and in some instances, older) welfare mothers trying to regain what they lost by having a child too early, causing them to miss out on life. I believe all of these things create a never-ending cycle. Our children have become products that continue to repeat the cycle. Even sadder, they are linked to not only the behavior of the mother but more so to the father who is not there.

It is interesting that diverse fathering behaviors have been associated or stereotyped to a particular ethnic or cultural group. Sigmund Freud used the term of "forgotten contributor." Absent African-American fathers by Freud would be considered a forgotten contributor – the invisible man and the sperm donor to a child's development.

The Bible speaks of generational iniquities that are passed down through the family bloodline. The sins of our fathers became a part of us before we were even born – the iniquities of the father being visited for several generations. This is how it is done and only the blood of Jesus can break it. If a blessing can be passed on, what makes us think a curse cannot be?

I was watching Oprah one day and they were discussing about how a child becomes a certain way. The psychologist stated parents have to take ownership for what they have done, either consciously or unconsciously. After I heard that I began to think that if the parent does this, it will definitely affect one's level of self-esteem. It will pour into the child a sense of worth by seeing the parent take ownership of behavior regardless of whether right or wrong. By not taking ownership, we are taking energy to preserve our attachment or detachment from our children, which sends out messages of how we are and how we feel about our children. The absent father undermines families, neglects children, causes or aggravates social problems (drugs, poverty, gangs, etc.) and interferes with an individual's happiness. The absent father generates an additional barrier that makes achievement harder. However, Freud also was quoted as saying "I cannot think of any need in childhood as strong as the need for a father's protection." If the father is not there, who protects the bastard, especially if she is a daughter?

Chapter 2
❧ A Historical Perspective ☙

*"And he shall go before him in
the spirit and power of Elias,
to turn the hearts of the fathers
to the children and the disobedient
to the wisdom of the just; to make ready
a people prepared for the Lord."*
~ Luke 1:17

The history of fatherhood has evolved so far from what was originally intended. Primarily fatherhood used to represent provider, head of household, caregiver and educator. Mother's role was very limited in the child's life, yet in her limitations she was the stabilizing force.

In this chapter we will explore the biblical and cultural perspectives of fatherhood. Evidence of cultures found puts an expression on the face of fatherhood. We can see a disconnect between our cultures' behavioral expectations for fathers and actual parental conduct throughout history.

With the story of Abraham, Sarah and Ishmael is where I will begin. In Genesis the 16th chapter, Sarah gets impatient waiting for the promise of God to manifest, so she offers her maidservant to Abraham. The 21st chapter of Genesis shows us God's promise to Sarah and then her fear of her handmaiden's son.

"Then Sarai, Abram's wife, took Hagar, her maid, the Egyptian, and gave her to her husband Abram to be his wife, after Abram had dwelt ten years in the land of Canaan. So he went to Hagar and she conceived." Genesis 16:3-4

"And the LORD visited Sarah as he had said, and the LORD did unto Sarah as he had spoken. For Sarah conceived, and bare Abraham a son in his old age, at the set time of which God had spoken to him.

And Abraham called the name of his son that was born unto him, whom Sarah bare to him, Isaac." Genesis 21:1-3

"And Sarah saw the son of Hagar the Egyptian, which she had born unto Abraham, mocking. Wherefore she said unto Abraham, Cast out this bondwoman and her son: for the son of this bondwoman shall not be heir with my son, even with Isaac. And the thing was very grievous to Abraham's sight because of his son. And God said unto Abraham, Let it not be grievous in thy sight because of the lad, and because of thy bondwoman; in all that Sarah hath said unto thee, hearken unto her voice; for in Isaac shall thy seed be called. And also of the son of the bondwoman will I make a nation, because he is thy seed. And Abraham rose up early in the morning, and took bread, and a bottle of water, and gave it unto Hagar, putting it on her shoulder, and the child, and sent her away; and she departed, and wandered in the wilderness of Beersheba.

And the water was spent in the bottle, and she cast the child under one of the shrubs. And she went, and sat her down over against him a good way off, as if were a bow shot; for she said, Let me not see the death of the child.

And she sat over against him, and lift up her voice, and wept. And God heard the voice of the lad; and the angel of God called to Hagar out of heaven, and said unto her, What aileth thee, Hagar? Fear not; for God hath heard the voice of the lad where he is. Arise, lift up the lad, and hold him in thine hand; for I will make him a great nation. And God opened her eyes, and she saw a well of water; and she went, and filled the bottle with water, and gave the lad drink. And God was with the lad; and he grew, and dwelt in the wilderness, and became an archer and he dwelt in the wilderness of Paran; and his mother took him a wife out of the land of Egypt." Genesis 21:9-21

The story of Ishmael's life begins with his conception in the 16th chapter of Genesis because of Sarai (who later becomes Sarah) rushed in an attempt to manifest the promise of God, and Abraham went along with her because he loved her. Even the greatest father in the Bible is not without blemish.

In the 21st chapter of Genesis, he then sends his firstborn out of the camp because of the fear of a woman, his wife. With this in mind, why should we think fathers of this age would be any different? The only difference is that Abraham was part of Ishmael's life through at least his teenage years; many men nowadays are lucky if they even see their teenage sons or daughters.

In the Roman times, the father's status as head of the household determined the child's status, whether a son or daughter. In Colonial America, the fathers carried the primary burden of raising the child, not the mother. In our early history there was a trend where it was a sin for a child to say he or she had no father. When the question was asked, *"Where is your father?"* and the response was "I do not have one," remarks from peers, church members and even adults brought shame, guilt and ridicule into the lives of such children. It finally got to the point that the majority of mothers would lie to the child by saying, *"Your father died in the war."* Now, the child believes and lives with the lie until the truth comes forth.

By the 19th century, the transition of the role of primary caregiver officially moved from father to mother, with even custodial guardianship shifting as well. In

1842, Reverend John S. C. Abbott wrote, *"Parental neglect is the ruin of many families."* Though he was talking during the wartime efforts, he was still basically saying we have made the single parent home the norm and it should not be that way.

Like Reverend Abbott, others believed fatherhood's fall from grace began due to the surfacing of the industrial revolution. During this period it was noted there were fewer property owners, longer work hours and fathers were no longer at the dinner tables. Mandatory schooling was enforced which further prevented fathers from spending time with and seeing their children. All of the above created a distance that denied the relationship development, so with it fell the responsibility of childrearing to the mother. Many historians believe this is the reason for the high rates of rejection, delinquency, abuse and illegitimacy.

In the late '70s and early '80s we went through a period where celebrity mothers made it a proud fact to be pregnant and unwed because they could choose to do so unaware of the natural and spiritual repercussions that would ensue. Many teenage girls began to think this was the "in" thing to do and teen pregnancy began to rise.

Check out these statistics from 1994 gathered from the United States Census Bureau:

- 1900 – 5% of children lived in single parent homes where the parent was divorced or never married.
- 1900 – 3.5% of children lived in one-parent homes where the parent was widowed.

- 1960 – 9% of children lived in single parent homes due to divorce or never married.
- 1992 – 5% of children lived in single parent homes where the parent was widowed.
- 1992 – 37% of children lived in single parent homes where the parent was divorced.
- 1992 – 36% of children lived in single parent homes where the parent never married.

Our individual cultures have always had slighted views of fatherhood. These views have played a significant role in the cultural upbringing of our children.

Asian-American Ethnicity

There are slight differences between the Chinese, Japanese, Korean and South Asian-Americans, which will not be discussed here. The Asian-American culture is viewed to be similar to the Latino-American culture. Most Asian-American families are patriarchal, family centered and male dominated. A high emphasis is placed on father-son relationships, and the father or eldest male exercises complete control over the entire household including servants. The father is viewed as the hard, dominant male figure while the mother is viewed as passive and dutiful. The mother is also viewed as self-sacrificing for her family, while the father is seen as the crucial foundation of power and authority. Though authority is vested in both parents, it is the father who has the final say. And the father is the key disciplinarian in the household.

Gender and age lines are firmly drawn in this culture. It is almost a sin for man not to have male child to carry on the family name. Recent studies suggest the Asian-American families are becoming more equal due to the mother's influence and her increased role of working outside of the home.

African-American Ethnicity

The father is almost non-existent or as Freud says *"invisible."* The men in the African-American culture were not normally viewed as weak or absent. It was only after being absorbed into the American culture that they were viewed as relatively weak, absent from home as well as from the day-to-day functioning of the family. The homes of most African-Americans are structured matriarchal, which has forced the woman to be self-reliant and self-sufficient, both during slavery and after slavery ended. Society states the African-American family is an unstable unit, shown by the signs of common law marriages and illegitimacy. African-American families have a tendency to be more controlling, strict and rigid than their other ethnic counterparts.

Marriages were not sanctioned during slavery and after slavery up to a certain point. However, many seem to forget African-American family patterns were destroyed with slavery and even more so dissolved when the slave owner sold the family separately to other slave owners because they were viewed as property. Most Americans at that time believed the African-Americans had no soul or feelings. So the only relationship left to be developed was between mother and child until one or the other were sold. Many studies have shown African-American families, when allowed to acquire power and property, develop the same patriarchal structure as that of the Anglo-American families.

Latino-American Ethnicity

The father in Latino-American culture is viewed as a dominant and authoritarian person. He is lord of his domain, while the wife is usually a gentle, submissive type. Fathers are considered to be macho men, who are proud and virile, yet they are to be respected and feared. They have been compared to African-American women who are strong and independent. The father has been viewed as aggressive and condescending at times, yet affectionate toward small children.

In the traditional image of the Latino-American families, the father's role is important and distinct by providing a positive influence in the lives of their children. Several studies noted the Latino-American families are not as rigidly structured as previously thought. In fact, Latino-American fathers have been found to be warm, nurturing and companionable when allowed to be.

Native American Ethnicity

The Native American culture is viewed as a single homogenous group even though there are about 280 tribal groups. The Native American family has been viewed as an *"incomplete"* Anglo-American family. The theory implies that the Native American family is not modern but simple, primitive. The older males or elders of the tribe were the relative male authority; however, women exercised a great power in the decision-making process, equal to that of the men. However, the more contact the Native Americans had with Anglo-Americans, the more the role of the women began to lessen. Similar to the Asian-American culture, the elders were respected, revered for their wisdom and their authority was considered to be sacred. In Native American cultures fathers are the ones who introduce their children, mainly their sons, to the world.

The Native American families were shocked by governmental policies and procedures, which played a hand in destroying the Native American culture. The different laws put into effect such as the Indian Child Welfare Act (1978) have caused major disorders of the families. The purpose of this act was that the government would, against the Native American's will, remove a Native American child from the family, place him or her in foster care, relocate them, and put them up for adoption based on social deficiency. The whole procedure could be done without due process and without letting the parents obtain legal counsel. My research showed this is the only culture where a child can be taken without due process.

It is also noted that as the Native American culture has begun to slip into the Anglo-American culture, many of the young are beginning to reject the traditional ways and questioning paternal authority. Children in Native American families are highly valued. Many family activities are done with them in mind. The family roots are more extensive than any other culture. The power and authority does not lie in a mother or a father but in the community as a whole. Though some tribes have converted to Christianity, most have retained their traditional practices and beliefs.

Society has long perceived that if a culture does not fit into the Anglo-American family format, then the culture was viewed as second-rate in societal beliefs. For many researchers the Anglo-American culture served as a benchmark by which other family forms have been measured. This served as the premise to determine the other structures were found to be lacking in their structures, not recognizing that all ethnic families do not fit into this pattern.

Latino and Asian-American fathers were viewed as authoritarian or un-American, more on the level of a dictator. African and Native American fathers have been viewed as absent, uninvolved, invisible, causing those societies to become more matriarchal. With all of this in mind, none of the cultures fits the "model" of the ideal Anglo-American family. The cultural forces have significantly shaped the father's role and how he executes within the family design.

Whether you are African-American, Latino-American, Asian-American, Native American or Anglo-American, there are always differences as well as similarities in the role of the father. As stated previously, there are some who believe if the model is not that of the Anglo-American, then it is inferior and doomed to failure. Sad to say, none of the previous cultures has been viewed as an adjustable and practical family unit by society's structured views.

When we consider all of these things, it is no wonder we cannot grasp the right way to be, and the hole in our soul continues to grow even bigger.

Chapter 3
❧ Being the Bastard ❦

*"No partner (person) in a love
relationship should feel that he
has to give up an essential
part of himself to make it
(the relationship) viable."*
~ May Sarton

I have always presented myself as being outwardly stable, confident and satisfied, while inwardly I felt silenced, afraid, stuck, doubtful, angry and hurt, yet unable to express those feelings. Though I strived for perfectionism, strangely I still felt powerless, without boundaries, overwhelmed by what was expected of me to carry out. I harbored fears of being left alone, of not taking risks and being in conflict with my inner man. I began to experience symptoms telling me my life was still missing something. There was this hidden persona I had denied and denied any effects it might have had on me. I had settled for being less than what I had the potential to be and did not know why. I had put that hidden persona to sleep and it had slept soundly, not wanting to be disturbed, but then the struggling began and it was yearning to be acknowledged.

It was once stated that the courts, society and churches were the causes of a father being unavailable, but the principle cause has always been the choice of the father. We confuse the term of being male or being a man with that of being a father. I have heard it said numerous times *"any man can make a baby but it takes a real man to be a father."* My question was *what does it take to be a bastard*? Nothing – just someone speaking it into your life. Being labeled a bastard penetrated my heart to the very depths of my being.

As men, sometimes you become concerned with your inability to love and to make a commitment. When this occurs then you begin to recognize the other areas such as anxiety, marriage, betrayal, abandonment, rejection and not finding someone to love you and for you to protect. These are the things, as women, we wish our fathers had. Like men, we then fear we have become failures and now everyone knows it. It is like having the scarlet letter imprinted on our forehead for all to see that we are the byproducts of our father's sin.

As defined earlier, a bastard is an illegitimate child, inferior and illegitimate in birth. It takes nothing on the child's part except to be born. You carry the stigma of your father's sin. You are the one labeled with it as if you are the one who did the wrong. You carry the label of the price that came because two consenting (and in some cases non-consenting persons) came into bodily contact on a more intimate level. Even as a bastard, I am aware part of my genetic structure, flaws and all, come from my father. I long to live in a culture where all men willingly accept, identify and empower their children. Do you have any idea what it is like to secretly suffer to such a great magnitude, carrying this shameful secret in your heart and being unable to release it into anyone's confidence?

Being born out of wedlock – not legitimate or unlawful – takes nothing on my part or that of another born in the same capacity, but society, relatives and friends label me as such, as if I were in the position of choosing to whom, where and how I was born. So amend the false words and broken promises – a child is produced, a bastard, one without legal rights, especially if the father takes no part in his or her life, or the mother refuses to name the father in order to protect the father for whatever reason. How many fathers (or even mothers) can say their children were actually conceived or born out of an act of love or just conceived out of a sexual, lustful act?

I believe I was the *"wild oat"* sown by my father, whether or not my parents *"truly"* loved each other, I know not for sure. I remember being at a Bible study one time and the teacher taught about "praying for a crop failure." That is for praying for things we did not want to stay in our lives. I was young, spiritually immature, and began to pray God would physically reverse my being a bastard. Now, I knew my father could not marry my mother because they were married to other people, but some part of me believed if God wanted to, He could change how the circumstances of my birth came about.

During this time of prayer I was watching a movie and in it the father went to court and had his illegitimate son's name changed legally to his, and I thought God that can happen for me and I would be "legal" and therefore I would be all right as a person. Excited about what had been revealed to me, I went and told my mother. After telling her, she took me into her arms and said, *"Though I understand your desire to have your father's last name, know this, there is no shame in having your grandfather's last name."* I realized she just did not understand my predicament. I wanted to be legal.

Many other bastards like myself have been or are in search of the father who knows how to love, guide, protect and provide, as well as encourage us to utilize our

God-given gifts to bring glory to God and fulfillment to ourselves. I heard it once said that a father who knows how to love, provide, protect and help teaches his daughter how to utilize her gifts. If an unsupportive or invisible father does nothing for building confidence and self-esteem in his "legitimate" child, he especially will not do it for the illegitimate one. A lack of a relationship with a father leaves a child unprepared and in unfamiliar territory, where the child must make a way for one's self no matter what the consequences.

The years a father spends with his child does have an effect on her. His relationship with her inspires her capacity to find a gratifying career, her intimate relationships and her spiritual foundations. William Appleton in his book, *Fathers and Daughters: A Father's Powerful Influence on a Woman's Life*, states a woman does not really begin to understand her relationship with her father until she is in her 30s.

I love my father and try to tell him often. My siblings from my mother and I have different fathers. I used to be so ashamed for people to know that tidbit of information and went to great lengths to not exactly lie, but cover up the truth by not implying what the situation at hand actually was. You know, the little *"white"* lie. I remember telling one of my best friends, Peggy O'Brien, the truth about my father. I remember as I told her, I felt so ashamed and tears started to flow. She comforted me and told me life is not perfect, and that my being illegitimate did not change her sisterly love for me and it would not make her think any less of me.

JAVA L. COLLINS

In my relationship with my father, the first sixteen
years of my life he spent denying my existence. Through
my half-sisters I learned how no one wanted to talk about
the first-born, the bastard. I had only seen him once during
that time frame when he bought my other sisters and
myself each a beach ball and a roll of gum. Later that year,
my stepmother sent me a bicycle for Christmas; this is the
only gift I have ever received in my life from my father,
even though it was my stepmother who sent it. However,
when God sent me that direction after the death of his
mother, my grandmother, I realized I was my father's sin
and wondered if every time he looked at me, did he revisit
the place of my creation, the place of his sin?

In the Bible there were altars erected to signify whether
a place was of God or sin, and I believe that in my father's
heart, he had subconsciously erected an altar to his sin. I
believe perhaps my existence to my father not only brought
confusion and worry, but it was confrontational and
challenging. This was evident one day as he introduced
me to a deacon friend in a neighboring county, who was
unaware he had a daughter older than the one he knew.
I watched as my father fidgeted trying, in a very subtle
way and with as few words as possible, to tell the man I
was his eldest daughter from a previous relationship. The
man's expression said it all as he replied "Oh!" I could
only imagine my father's distress and shame at having to
give an explanation for my presence. While staying with
my dad for six months, everyone thought I was there for
the money, an inheritance, when actually all I wanted was

to be loved and accepted by him, my stepmother, and my siblings – to make a sense of connection with them, a sense of belonging; this was the inheritance I was after.

A question that constantly nagged at me was *how could I be a complement to the fulfillment of God's plan, if my father were not there doing his part*? Many fathers had limited personal contact with their child, which unfortunately as a bastard daughter turned into a "no access" card in a male-dominated world.

When a father leads a wayward life that potential for the same life lies like a seed dormant in the child. When light comes, or knowledge is recognized or given, it is up to the child to purpose whether or not that potential will spring forth. And more often than not, the seed of the wayward is often what takes control.

Fathers who are distant, absent, or invisible are unable to form any type of relationship with their children. There were times when I found myself starved for affection and felt emotionally inept. When I got married I did not know how to be a woman, wife and mother because of the hole left in me. I had no father, though I had father figures, to learn much from and had to learn to rely on myself and on the information (albeit sometimes inaccurate) from my mother and her female friends. This is a true part of my own relationship with my father. As long as I do not need anything from him, he is okay, but if I call him to ask for help he will make excuses and be disappointed in me. He once told me (though I was older at the time) that he was trying to raise me so I could have a home, a car and a job with benefits before I turned 50. Where was this much-needed advice when I was in my teens? When I needed him most? Fathers, do not wait until your children are grown up to try and raise them, but meet them where they are and begin to impart into their lives.

Being a father, whether active or passive, will have a life-changing effect on a child. Once a father becomes involved and displays a caring, loving attitude, it helps promote the child's well being. A father needs to show affection, show his love at all times to his wife and children. This display of intimacy causes two things to occur: 1) it tells the child you want to be around him or her and 2) it shows you want to impart a foundation for the child. There should be a desire to build a foundation, but not just any foundation – a firm godly foundation which leaves the child with a Godly heritage.

If you do not remember anything else in this book remember this: I found myself suffering and frustrated which made me determined to change my bastard status. *Suffrage and frustration will motivate in you the desire to change.* After looking over my life, I saw all the wrong turns; you know the ones: the unhappy marriage, stupid love affairs that went nowhere, feelings of insecurity, repeated failure in a career or relationships – all these things caused pain and I needed to know what would alter this unhappy pattern. In order to change, I had to recognize there had to be alternative ways to behave and feel. I did possess the power to change my status and myself. Although the desire for change is good, it is useless unless you are willing to put some effort and determination behind it to make the change in your life occur. I was more than ready.

I discovered through my own study, that in God's eyes I am legal and I do have an inheritance, but during my hunt for belonging, none of that mattered at the time. I wanted to delete, erase and destroy the legacy of brokenness left behind by my natural father, which flowed so freely through my lineage. I did not want this cycle to be repeated, for this was not the type of inheritance I wanted to leave for my son.

As I said, I love my father, but unless the love of a father is given to us, then myself and others like me, are denied the love we crave and will not be content or satisfied because we are searching to fill the void, the hole in us, some other way.

"Unfortunately . . his (a father's) behavior sends
a message that, that is what he thinks of her,
so she comes to believe it herself."
~ Nicky Marone (1989)
How to Father a Successful Daughter

Chapter 4
☙ Emotionally Raped ☙

*"The wealth of a soul is measured by
how much it can feel;
its poverty by how little."*
~ William R. Alger

A father can be of a major influence in his children's lives, especially his daughters, but his lack of influence and a relationship can handicap her in more ways than one. It affects her developmental growth. During the child development transition, fathers have had a hard time anchoring what they say with sincerity and sometimes integrity. His inability to speak about certain things, especially his emotional realities, can become a woman's silence, meaning it shuts us down to the point we say nothing or begin to become someone who we were not meant to be.

When a father denies sharing his emotions – his being – he begins to develop a child who is less whole, less unique and full of **limited** possibilities. He is denying his child the love, respect and validation from one of the two people who matter the most in his or her life. The child's potential is now compromised because of her father or his invisibility. Sigmund Freud once said *"I cannot think of any need in childhood as strong as the need for a father's protection."* When a father does not pour into his child, this denial develops within us an impoverished soul.

As a woman I viewed the rejection, the lack of acceptance, of not belonging as something I had done, not realizing the wounding had been done by my father. His invisible presence had created feelings of insecurity, detachment and isolation. This left me feeling emotionally raped. It left me feeling unworthy to expect love, warmth, closeness, and even being wrong to desire intimacy. I had failed to learn these qualities are not always evident in men. As a wounded woman I **reacted** by being withdrawn. I know other women who have reacted by being sexually promiscuous, frigid, or being excessively angry. I realized in my relationships, the few I have had, I wanted and began to demand total devotion and when the criteria was not met, I blamed myself and took one of two approaches: 1) I would look for a way to end the relationship, in which case the cycle began again, or 2) I would stay in it, feeling I got what I deserved, that this was my fate, my lot in life. Eventually, I did begin to learn to grow up and realize that being alone was not the end of the world. When confronted or challenged with situations we can choose to react or respond; now I know how to respond and not let my actions cause me to react.

One night I was watching a documentary on television dealing with primates. The show focused on how the males or fathers were more involved with the infant primate's care. What was interesting was that if the infant lost its father, a male from another tribe would *"adopt"* the infant, assuming total care for it, and by doing so this increased the infant's chances of survival. Why is it that animals in the wild exhibit more sense than those made in God's image?

My father, like many others, did not realize he had the power to build up a child or blast and cripple one. This is so astounding! They do not know their absence has created deep resentments in us, wrapped in a lot of hurt and pain. By my father not pouring into me, his daughter, his first born, he started an *assassination of my future.* He was an assistant in destroying my worth and damaging my perception. The hole in me left a part of my life injured, wounded and underdeveloped.

Now you are probably asking *when are you going to take responsibility for yourself?* I am and I have, but I had to acknowledge where the *hole* came from. There are other areas, but I believe when a father does not impart unto his children especially his daughters, there is an emptiness, which a woman, mainly a mother, cannot fill. Mother was not designed to be the head of the home, father was but this make up was changed in the Garden of Eden. When God asked Adam who gave him the fruit to eat, his response was *this woman You gave me,* and he blamed it on the woman. At that point, I believe spiritually and physically, Adam handed over his role as head of the family to woman.

Sexual and physical abuse does not make for good fathering and it is on the rise because of a lack of fathering, or as my pastor put it in his book, *The Blended Families,* because no one is looking and everyone is being selfish about his or her own needs. Being sexually and emotionally abused, the word father began to have little or no meaning to me. This attack on my innocence left me *"emotionally challenged."* I would get around men and could only feel distrust. My perception of whom or what a father was became distorted as I recalled my memory of what a father had done. I had no connection to closeness, trust or love, I had been emotionally raped and my intellect and heart reflected it. Later, I learned this is why I could not view God as a loving, gracious and merciful Father. I thought He would only treat me right if I were good.

James Alan McPherson, a professor at the University of Iowa, in his book *Fathering Daughters: Reflections by Men*, summed up part of how I felt.

"The real tragedy of the history of Black Americans is that we are shaped in part by the structures that constantly abuse us . . . The prisoner always knows more about the prison keeper. . . But the deeper human tragedy is that the prisoner, . . . runs the risk of becoming like him (the prison keeper) . . ."

I understood this to say that once I become so much like my father I run the risk of being my father. He further states that this *freezes the flow of human emotions into habits of the mind that have been already proven to be destructive.* The tragedy of the cycle continues.

Often I wondered if my father felt the terrible loss I felt from him not being a part of my life. Did he realize his invisibility during the major years of my life deprived me of stability in my relationships? His absence almost brought a halt to my developmental advancement because of my constant struggle with issues of security, love and trust? These issues I struggled with I tried hard not to pass onto my son, thereby placing him at a disadvantage in his adolescence.

When a father fails to value his daughter, he in fact is rejecting her femininity which affects her growth as a woman. I believe this is one of the reasons teen pregnancies are on the rise. As a daughter she has no one to teach her, so she goes looking for fatherhood on her own, which often is met with tragic results, especially in her relationships with men.

I would have dreams often as a child and even as an adult about being raped and being powerless to do anything about it and I would silently pray for someone to come and save me, but no one would ever come. So, I would finally surrender to my attacker, feeling all was hopeless and praying he would kill me and not let me live with the burden of what was being committed. *My point is that being fatherless made me feel powerless.* Being a bastard made me feel I had no rights and the rapist could do whatever he wanted because he was in authority, in control, and was able to get away with it.

During the short time I stayed with my father, it was not until two months later that I realized the damage done to me. I found myself ill, becoming scared and lonely. I could feel myself starting to withdraw into myself – what if I could not find another job, no healthcare, no car, no home and no savings? What if the words my father had spoken became true? As I looked in his eyes, I saw failure and had almost resigned myself to being what he said and with nothing more. I let his actions and words diminish the value I had placed on my life. Why? Because I was looking for a father, my father – I had chased the dream, and then his spoken words produced in me a shattering. This insight showed how my faith in God had been shattered and made me see how I could not see God as my Father. Since I had disappointed my father, I knew

I had disappointed God as well. This showed me how powerful, how influential a father's role is in the life of a child. Once again, I had been emotionally raped.

When I was younger, I would have this dream of seeing a baby on the couch with a bottle propped up with a pillow. I would say in the dream *"Poor baby, why doesn't someone come and tend to you?"* With no one around I wondered if the baby could survive. Later I shared the dream with my mother who looked at me strangely and then said, *"How could you remember that? We had to lay you down during your feeding time because the doctor said you weren't thriving. Always after you ate you would throw up and become dehydrated, on the verge of having to be hospitalized."*

I was barely six weeks old when that happened. Every time I was held during feeding time, I would throw up everything. My mother was not able to bond with me and didn't know how to bond with me during the alternative feeding time; this assisted in the creation of the beginning of the hole in my soul. I lacked the nurturing most babies received during those critical months after birth; I was denied. Still, I would not connect the dots until much later in my life. I had always had strong feelings of detachment, rejection and abandonment, but as I entered my late twenties and early thirties they intensified. It was not until I went through a healing session that I was able to make the connection with the baby in the dream. My child within was struggling to be whole, to have the ties of bondage cut away, struggling to be free.

Chapter 5
❧ Struggling to be Whole ❧

"In our deepest moments of struggle,
frustration, fear, and confusion,
we are being called upon to reach in
and touch our hearts.
Then we will know what to do,
what to say, how to be . . ."
~ Roberta Sage Hamilton

The child within struggles because she is separated from her passion – which is her treasure, her purpose. What started out as a joke or playing has caused the child within much distress and as we become adults instead of addressing the hole, we choose to try and fill it with other things, hoping they will do the trick. I believe when a person begins to self-search for his or her purpose, it is the child within who holds the key for seeking the treasure from which he or she was separated. The father represents the key to wholeness for the struggling child. The father is the one she can go to and he will help her find the lost treasure. He is the one expected to slay the dragons and monsters while the child is on her quest to pursue that which is lost or hidden. She is the princess and he is the king who would risk his kingdom for his daughter. When it is dark and she cannot see, he provides the light to guide her.

His wisdom in her life situations were meant to build her character, give her direction and help her realize she is too important for God's purpose for her life to be destroyed. However, the lack of the father's willingness to intervene and be a part of his child's life has left the child struggling to be whole.

As I said earlier, I went to spend some time with my father and during my time there I recalled a scene from my **very first** visit with my father. I remember being excited when I first met my father; my stepmother had taken us all Easter shopping, and I excitedly showed my father my purchase. He looked at me with a blank stare as if to say *so what*, then continued explaining to a gentleman friend what he wanted him to do. I felt so crushed! As my father's first born, this was not the response I was expecting him to give me. From that point on I never shared any of my accolades with him because his response said he did not care.

My father failed to affirm me. So I became what I heard one author call a *"armored Amazon,"* especially after my husband and I divorced. I assumed the masculine functions of fathering to be both mother and father and to cover up my pain. However, this pseudo-masculine shell brought on against the pain of abandonment and rejection, protected my soft feminine posterior. I was protecting its vulnerability. When a father validates a daughter he, in fact, is actually blessing her and this blessing produces confidence, courage and boldness.

When I mentor young girls I try to instill in them some droplets because I know I am not their father, or mother for that matter, nor am I trying to be; but if I can help close the hole a little, then it is worthwhile. Many fathers unknowing, even if they live in the home, wound their daughters. That father can be unable to hold a job, is an alcoholic, a drug addict, a workaholic, abusive and can deny his daughters the benefit of growing up whole.

After going to stay with my father for a while as an adult, I got sick and since my mother had died from heart disease, perhaps the family did not want me to die from the same thing, especially being with them. This is not to say they were not concerned about my welfare, but I began to feel heartbroken, to sense my own father did not want me around. How did I know? His actions toward me began to imply what he found wrong with how my mother had raised me. This angered me especially when, in my opinion, he began to talk down to me about the way my mother raised me. My thoughts were *"Here was a man who knew where I was for sixteen years and still denied my existence, and now he was being critical of my mother's childrearing abilities. Here is a man who when I graduated from high school did not even offer to help me go to college."* I caught myself because I was at risk of saying *"at least my mother did not abandon me and pretend I did not exist."* Who wants a father who will only accept you when you do as he says? You become raised with the mentality of risking his wrath, and no matter how odd the reason, you think this is love, the love of a father.

Strong disappointment began to stir in me; I had to face the fact that my father was unable to satisfy my needs for a father. His attempt to stand as a father in my eyes had been shaken to the point of being almost destroyed. I felt a lack of compassion or acceptance by this person, this man, who fathered me. Reality finally replaced the fantasy, the wishful thinking.

To my father I had no value unless I had my own car, my own money, my own house and my own job with benefits. He could not imagine or understand my being obedient to God and viewed my illness as a curse that would rob him of his money and time. It was interesting that one night I could not sleep and as I prayed I heard the voice of God say, *"Did you find what you were looking for? Is this the inheritance you want? That you believed you deserved? Is this what you are fighting for?"* At the same time Bishop Eddie Long came on television and I heard him say, *"That God trusted some fathers to carry the seed, but He didn't trust them to raise it."* As I prepared to leave my father's home and return to my mother's home, I realized I was coming full circle. I finally smiled as I thanked God that my earthly father carried the seed, but God, my heavenly Father, raised it.

When my paternal grandfather developed Alzheimer's, I realized then more than ever I wanted to try and build a relationship with my father before he forgot who I was. I did not understand my father was trapped in his own negative behavior patterns, which had been brought on by his upbringing. I began to realize one of my flaws – or strengths depending on how one viewed it – was that I had a tendency, as I got older, to challenge authority, especially if it incorporated changes that did not involve input from those it affected. And to make matters worse, I would later begin to feel guilty about doing what was right. When a father does not take his rightful place in his daughter or son's life, the balance and respect for authority is not instilled within.

I took ownership of my being resentful that my life was so difficult and no longer blamed what I had not received from my father as to what was wrong in my life. When I am uncomfortable or in unnerving situations, like many others, I shift my feelings and attitudes to that person, when in actuality I was transferring my past to my present instead of dealing with it.

There are times I still struggle with the fear of making the same mistakes over and over, of going around the mountain until I am on a sightseeing excursion, of being stuck. There was a time when I let my fears consume my desires; I let them consume my dreams. The old fears would arise, bringing with it a fresh flood of new fears. Then I realized I am doing myself a disservice by allowing the fears to keep me from my dreams, my desires, my purpose, by allowing the hole in my soul to drain me dry.

I was missing a piece of my *"self."* I felt I was somehow not whole and complete. Though true, in a sense, I had to come and see myself as whole and complete, but with missing pieces and broken parts. I had a choice to make and I was willing to look back over my life. The first thing I saw that came to my mind were the regrets and the sad times. Do you see the pieces of yourself lying along the path of your life? The ones where you did not feel good enough, or where you were criticized or blamed by someone else? Slowly, I began to ask *where was the good*? Surely, there was something good, some good memories? Have you ever stopped to look at the memories of when you won the prize, felt really great, on top of the world – those moments that prove what a wonderfully amazing human being you are? So, I looked at my memories and found the good, those I knew made me feel on top of the world.

When I made my choice to no longer let myself be unwhole, God led me to a church where I could be healed, accepted and not discarded. He led me to a man who knew how to be a father and could teach me how to be a daughter. *It is the love of a father who helps his daughter gain confidence in who she is, gaining in her independence and developing a sense of not only being worthy of love, but entitled to it and capable of loving herself.*

Chapter 6
❧ The Abuse of Spiritual Authority ❧

*"Becoming mature means learning to accept
what you cannot change, facing unresolved sorrows . . .
and part of loving life is admitting your regrets."*
~ Barbara Sher

Abuse means *to misuse; to use wrongly or improperly; to deceive; to malign (to speak ill of, having an evil disposition).* Abuse. It takes many forms – physical, emotional, sexual, verbal, neglect, substance, spiritual. Abuse can be either one of these alone or a combination of any or all forms of them. Abuse, like drugs, alcohol, smoking, etc., knows not any sex, ethnic background and economic or social status. From personal experience, I can tell you abuse can strike whether you are in a two-parent or single-parent home.

Abuse means *to misuse; to use wrongly or improperly; to deceive; to malign (to speak ill of, having an evil disposition).* Abuse. It takes many forms – physical, emotional, sexual, verbal, neglect, substance, spiritual. Abuse can be either one of these alone or a combination of any or all forms of them. Abuse, like drugs, alcohol, smoking, etc., knows not any sex, ethnic background and economic or social status. From personal experience, I can tell you abuse can strike whether you are in a two-parent or single-parent home.

Though physical abuse is the most obvious, emotional, neglect and spiritual abuse are harder to define. Either way, all types of abuse produce pain on different levels and in different ways. Contrary to what some would like to think, abuse does not just happen. If you are brought up seeing abuse, you will begin to think this is normal in a relationship. The person doing the abuse will most of the time justify his or her reasoning for being abusive. At times, recognizing abuse may be difficult, especially for the victim or victims. No one wants to believe someone they love would actually intentionally hurt them, but it happens. Know this, it is important to recognize any type of abuse is not normal, is not healthy, is not acceptable and definitely is not the fault of the person who is being abused.

Even spiritually, an abuser can manipulate us. Many of us who are or have been abused begin to distrust others. We become angry, bitter and in some cases, frightened. We feel unloved, alone, rejected, abandoned, unworthy. Self-doubt becomes our constant companion and it is whom we reach out to for comfort instead of human contact. We accept the abuse as our fault, feeling there was something we had done or did that brought this on us.

In light that many cases of spiritual abuse are now coming forward at an alarming rate, it is something we cannot pretend any longer that it does not exist. There were times when dirt in the church was swept under the covers by payment, reassignment of clergy, etc. Now, it is everywhere in the media: priest molests boys, pastor fathers child outside of marriage, pastor beats wife, pastor caught in an adulterous affair or sexual activity.

Though I could go into great details on abuse, the focus of this chapter deals with spiritual abuse, whether from a person in authority over you or your own spiritual father. I have heard it said, "You have not known hurt, until you have been spiritually hurt by someone in the church;" this is an old saying that holds a major truth. Spiritual abuse damages you to the point where the victim is faced with one of three major choices, though there could be more: 1) bury it internally and ignore it; 2) leave the church (you either church hop or drop out altogether); or 3) look at what happened, examine it, forgive and get yourself free.

Many times those in spiritual positions of authority will feel they are doing you a favor by talking down to you, point out your shortcomings in public or in front of a few others or by blowing up and blasting you and everyone else. They never apologize because they feel as a servant of God they have done their part, and feel justified (in the flesh, of course) that what they did was right and God approved.

When we join a church, we are openly yielding ourselves to those in authority over us. We trust them with our spiritual growth, our spiritual well-being. So when a spiritual father abuses his position of authority, especially in our lives, it sends us running for cover or walking around wounded, acting as if nothing is wrong. The effects most of the time are devastating. We have been taught to quote the Word and use it toward the enemy, but not how to protect ourselves from those we love spiritually who are hurting us.

Those who are in a position of spiritual authority have a responsibility to build up those under them. Abuse will damage your congregation, especially those who are serving. It reduces us to a fraction of a shell of ourselves. A private war begins to rage on the inside of us, and it is very real. We find ourselves struggling to take the fragments of our now shattered spiritual being and hold them together by any means necessary. The darts of self-doubt, feeling foolish and unworthy, strike constantly to tear down that which had been built up.

In my situation, I did not know what to expect from a spiritual father and for a moment felt I had no need for one. However, I found myself desiring one because I realized my father was not a covering for me. A spiritual father in my eyes carries the same weight, if not more, than a natural father. The importance of a spiritual father bears mentioning.

As I stated earlier, my natural father did not raise me, though I had more than my share of stepfathers (not that there is anything wrong with having one). My stepfathers never really were "fathers"; they were more like friends or acquaintances. There was no protection, no fun, no security, or no love. They did nothing to build my self-esteem, confidence, or prepare me to be who I was destined to be; most of the time they kept their distance.

In the latter part of 1st Corinthians 9:18 Paul says, ". . . *I may make the gospel of Christ without charge, that I abuse not my power in the gospel.*" Paul recognized that the calling to a position of spiritual authority came with a price to impart to and protect those whom he was over. When a spiritual father steps over into the abuse realm, the repercussions are major. Just like when a pebble is thrown into the water, it will always produce a ripple, no matter how big or small. The same is with abuse.

As I said in my situation, I did not know what to expect from a natural father, let alone a spiritual one. I had been to several churches looking for a father-like spiritual leader. At one point I had a person in authority, whom I greatly respected, tell me I had an ugly, black spirit. The way it was said left no room to doubt the person meant the words. The tone in which the words were spoken contained such disgust and malice; those words left me walking wounded for almost three years. This was not the first time this person had said something to me along these lines, but the impact of those words were like a rope around my neck. I felt like I was struggling to live, though every time I saw the person, my goal was, as always, to treat him with respect, even though he abused his position of authority in my life.

My healing took place when I found my spiritual father and to this day I thank God for him rescuing me. I was on the verge of leaving my faith because the pain was unbearable. I watched this man with a very discerning eye because I did not want to be hurt again. After a few months of watching him and being in his presence, I realized he truly believed what he spoke, acted on it and dared anyone to say otherwise. I knew I had found a father-like leader to heal, to guide and speak life into my weary, dried up soul. Yes, there are times my spiritual father may say or ways he may act which will cause me to think he does not love me or has hurt my feelings, but I get over it; and if it is bad enough I go to him and talk. My prayer is that every wounded soul would be as blessed as I am to find a spiritual father of such integrity. My spiritual father used his position of authority to rebuild, restore and revive the devastated places in my life.

The problem is that in the church, no one is trained to recognize *spiritual abuse*, so therefore it goes unchecked and is on a rampage until the one in authority either lines back up with the Word of God and changes, or the person's shame becomes a public disgrace. If you feel you have been a victim of spiritual abuse, like with the other forms of abuse – tell someone. Your healing, your sanity, your spiritual redemption depends on it.

Getting help and support to change your situation is a must. You may even find yourself with lingering, painful emotions that your mind keeps recalling; cover yourself with the blood and remind yourself – you are more than a conqueror through Christ Jesus. Take courage and begin the process to rebuild feelings of self – safety, confidence and esteem.

Chapter 7
⮞ A Reason to Live ⮜

*"Treasure your relationships,
not your possessions."*
~ Anthony D'Angelo
from The College Blue Book

Parents tend to forget that when children are brought into this world it is not because they asked to be born. Therefore, they should become the most important people in our lives. However, we have a tendency to treat them like they are the least important. We treat them with the least amount of respect, trust and kindness. I have a very strong dislike for the phrase *"Children should be seen and not heard."* For this is how we treat our children. Many of us get to the point that we just tolerate them, wishing they would grow up, especially once they pass the stage we like. Our patience with them gets short. We do not take the time to watch the tone in which we speak to them or the words that come out of our mouths.

Words can kill a child's spirit quicker than anything. The damage is done to the psyche, sense of self, sense of well-being, sense of love. We loose control with them, then demand they control themselves! They control themselves? When we are the ones who have lost it. I believe the drama of our own lives and the drama of the lives of our parents cause us to hurt, to leave, to abandon, or even reject our children.

My reason for living is tied to me finding my worth, my value. My worth is tied to that which my father, as well as others, has imparted to me. When the father is invisible, no relationship is established. Love has failed me. It has affected my self-esteem, so it has provided yet another obstacle, another barrier, for me to overcome to enhance my life.

I noticed that as a person, when I am insecure I keep people at a distance. For I know that at a distance, the damage they can do to me is minimal, but once they get close, the damage can be catastrophic. When people disappoint me, I pull away. When people use me, I pull away. William Appleton stated that *self-esteem was made of self-confidence*. He believed it contained the conviction *that one is competent to judge, think and correct one's mistakes, competence and self-respect*. In other words, I had the ability to feel worthy within me.

I believe part of the hole in my soul is due to the fact I was deprived of my father's love and attention. Without this, I developed low self-esteem due to some "perverted" fatherhood images in my life; however, though I find it easy to love and accept others, I had trouble loving and accepting myself. The reality is if I have trouble loving and accepting myself, then I really have problems loving and accepting others. When a child feels a sense of belonging from both parents, it is only then that she stands the chance of becoming whole.

Slowly I began to realize a few things about my life. When I became frustrated due to having no challenges, talents falling by the wayside, low salaries and a need for accomplishment, it affected my confidence in myself. I am a well-educated woman who desires and believes she deserves more money, has a sense of purpose, wants greater responsibility and needs to be innovative. Even wanting revenge for a wrong done made me doubt my worth as a person.

I realized I changed jobs because I was restless and lost interest after accomplishing certain things. I needed to possess the strength to create a balance between my needs and those my career demanded of me. I wanted to live by artful skill, while asserting assurance, confidence, and authority.

All of the above was rooted in my denial of my *paternal investment* into my life. On my father's behalf there was in the physical a lack of protection, provision, character building and nurturing. On the spiritual side there was a lack of protection, provision, instilling character, value and impartation into my womanhood. I was allowed to be raised in a world *without knowledge of my past, undervaluing my present, and misunderstanding my future.* Knowledge is gained by experience. If parents – especially fathers – fail to acknowledge and admit their faults, then they have failed to learn from the lessons of their mistakes, thereby perpetuating the cycle. What goes around comes around and around and around until someone is bold enough to make a stand for change.

My reason to live was blocked up, held back because I had no idea of who I really was. My fear of rejection, abuse, abandonment and illegitimacy held me hostage. I was preventing the true expression of my being from coming forth. The question that plagued me was: *Is it worth it, trying to overcome the "bastard" status to achieve something worthwhile in my life?* Yes!

As I was contemplating this book, I remembered I used to tell my son all the time he was my favorite son, and that he could do anything, he was a wise and smart son, and I loved him very much. Being the wise and smart son, he proved it one day. I was in the process of telling him he was my favorite child and he stopped me, took my face in his hands and said, *"Mom, I'm your only son, in fact, I'm your only child!"* He was about five years old when he told me that and my response to him was, *"I still mean what I said to you."* I believe to this day those words are tattooed in his heart. They are tied to his sense of worth and value of himself. A word of caution here is that when you are raising a child(ren) of value and worth, be careful with whom you leave them. Sometimes, unknowingly, those you trust will undermine what you are trying to build in your child(ren), causing a crack in their armor or their safety net. It will rear its head later and cause your child to begin to doubt the words spoken to him or her as a child, consequently creating a whole new scenario to build again.

I once heard it said that *the highest image of self promotes wholeness in spirit, soul and body.* The strength of my spirit, soul and heart are what invoked the possibility of change in me to occur and gave me the reason to live.

Chapter 8
❧ A Father's Love ❧

*"Love and respect are
the most important aspects
of parenting, and of all relationships."*
~ Jodie Foster (Actress)

A father's love should bring a balance into the lives of his children. It is fundamental for them to develop good and healthy – mentally, emotionally, physically and spiritually. A father needs to contribute to the development of his fruit – his children, so they may experience wholeness.

A real father is giving and generous. Remember the story of the Prodigal Son in Luke chapter 15, verses 11-32. The son goes to the father and asks for his inheritance so he may go and see the world. The son extravagantly spent all his wealth and when he had no more, he found out he also had no more friends. So he went to work for a farmer and was eating the food left over in the pigs' trough when the thought hit him that his father had much and would hire him; he remembered his father's hired hands ate better than this. So he returned home, not knowing that every day since he had left, his father had been looking for him to return. When the son returned home, the father ordered the fattest calf killed and a feast prepared; he put on his son a ring and robe, rejoicing that he was home. How we wish our fathers would do the same for us. Show us that kind of father's love. A real father builds up his child's character, not by damaging it or tearing it down.

The hole in your soul can be heart shattering. Traditionally we are taught that healthy human development in a person is noticed when a self-sufficient, independent person stands before you. However, this is usually what is expected of men and not women. This view in itself is interesting seeing that mothers, not fathers, mainly raise us.

I believe we have a natural, innate connection to our mothers, but the connection to our fathers must be nurtured. We act as mirrors, reflecting those we tend to be around the most. If the father is not around, how is it we imitate his actions? Half of our genes are his. Just because we may look like him does not necessarily mean we are a reflection of him. With no father to provide protection, provision, consistency and stability the way God structured it, it is no wonder we are full of holes. We have been deprived of what should have been rightfully imparted unto us by our fathers.

The realization came upon me; I had unjustly imposed the responsibility of fatherhood upon my previous spiritual leaders and other father figures. I wanted from them what I could not get from my natural father and when the promise of it manifesting dissipated, I became upset not just naturally but spiritually. I felt betrayed when I felt my situation warranted more than godly advice or prayer and neither was offered, especially after reaching out but the response in return was not what I wanted nor was it what I had anticipated. This reaction profoundly had an impact on my self-esteem. Realizing I was searching for acceptance from God through those He placed in authority over me and when abuse came, I accepted it because I thought this was a way to be loved and please God. Everything soon left me wondering if I would find what I was looking for. Without a father present, take it from me, your sons and your daughters will look elsewhere to discover an example of fatherhood which will lead them to believe what they find represents an example of manhood, too. Another drawback that happens is you no longer face life, but continue to run away when it gets too hard.

Upon reading First Corinthians 13, better known as the Love chapter, I would use that as a measuring stick to see if I were worthy of love. If I had missed it in at least two areas, then I deemed myself not worthy of love and if I were not worthy to love myself, then neither God nor my father would love me. The standards by which we were raised caused us to set our own invisible standard to be met or exceeded.

When I arrived at Covenant Family Church, I was wounded, broken, betrayed and locked up. My intent was to sit in the congregation and not do a thing. I was positive that if I would sit still and ride this out, I would be okay. I knew I had been led to that church, but I was still thinking maybe I should go somewhere else, but that was not to be the case. The senior pastor even went on to say if you are here, it is because God has led you this way.

My sister Demetria, who was a volunteer at the church, started asking me to go with her to help out. Though I really did not want to, I went. I was comfortable with the assistant pastor because she and I attended a previous church together, but whenever the senior pastor came I was looking for a place to hide. He would do small talk, which really was not small talk for him because he is a very direct and to-the-point type of person.

One day he stopped by the desk where we were and I sat there trying my best not to get into a conversation with him and my sister. Finally my sister blurted out *"Pastor, she's looking for a father."* I wanted to kill her and just tell God she died on her own. Since I could not do that, I smiled a small smile and kept doing whatever it was I was doing. He nodded and then left. On his way out of the office, he came by and touched my shoulder and said, *"I am looking for a daughter."* He smiled and left. He, to this day has no idea how just those few words impacted my heart, for even in his words I felt the love of a father and thought *God is this what it feels like to have Your love?*

During my prayer time, God showed me that if I watched and observed the man of God, He promised to show me the love of a father. By doing that I have had the opportunity to get a taste of what I had been searching for all those years. I am having the opportunity for the hole in my soul to be filled. This is a process and will take time, but *I am willing to give it the time that is required in exchange for wholeness.* It is because of my desire for wholeness that I think about the *"lost generation"* coming up –those whose lifestyles are driven by gang violence, drugs and abuse of all types. I believe they are a remnant I want to reach out to. Without guidance, teenage fathers are doomed to repeat the fatherless cycle. Some theorists say teenage fathers have been neglected and given a distorted public image – that their roles in teen pregnancies have presented a misleading sketch of them. Though some truth may ring in this, still the cycle needs to be broken.

I once heard in my spirit: *worldly men, wise men, rulers and kings*. I asked God what did that mean? He said **the men who seek the world become worldly, but men who seek wisdom become rulers and kings.** After thinking on this for a few days, it did not take long for me to realize I wanted to be a ruler, a king; this was resonating inside of me and yearning to break free.

In the previous chapter I stated hearing Bishop Eddie Long say *God trusted some fathers to carry the seed but not to raise it*. As I look over things now, I am really grateful that my earthly father carried the seed, but God raised me. The assassination attempt on the ruler, the king inside of me, would have surely perished. I love my father with all my heart and take nothing from him. He could only do what he knew to do. I realized he had not been raised in an atmosphere to do what should have been natural to him. Many fathers are this way and there comes a point where we have to release them from what they did not know.

The question we should be asking is: *What is expected of fathers, what do we want from them, not only on personal terms but social ones as well*? In the colonial period, fathering was a devoted and revered position. A father took pure delight in the birth of his child and suffered grievously at its death. Using old cultural ideas of fatherhood to level out the new ideas will not enlighten us. It is better to understand how fathers can move from passive to active, to getting involved with their child's life.

Modernization has caused fatherhood to deteriorate. It is only now in the present day that a deliberate effort is being made to build up emotional security in a family, with the father having an active part. Many new studies are treating the aspect of fatherhood as if it is something newly discovered, instead of the "sperm donor" mentality.

In present times, a father's role is very much starting to change. It is going beyond that which was traditionally structured (provider, breadwinner, disciplinarian, etc.). It is becoming a commonplace thing to see fathers displaying affection, being intimate with their children as well as receiving intimacy from them.

An unknown author once wrote, *"Precious thought, my Father knoweth, in His love, I rest, For whate'er my Father doeth. Must be always best."* I believe with the love of a father, this generation will not be lost and can be turned around for the glory of God.

JAVA L. COLLINS

"The Lord Jehovah is my strength and my song;
He also is my salvation."
~ Isaiah 12:2

Chapter 9
❧ Letting Go: The Act of Forgiveness ❧

"Forgiveness means you've
decided not to keep festering . . .
(it) is a powerful yet challenging tool
that will support and honor you.
At the core of the heart, you have
the power to move beyond the old
issues that are still hindering your freedom."
~ Doc Childre and Howard Martin
The HeartMath Solution

There is a part of me that wants to cling to the illusions and imaginations of wishful thinking, of the what-ifs, yet the other part – the stronger part – aches for strength to make my life better. I want to not only see but also be the person I really am destined to be.

The Bible in Genesis 2:3 says God made me in His image and many Christians believe fatherhood to be an emulation of God the Father. So is it possible that without a father, I can still be a reflection of God the Father? Is it possible that I can release the feelings of hurt, rejection and abandonment, of not being good enough or worthy enough to be called daughter by my father? Is it possible that I can exchange all of that and forgive him, my mother, myself? Yes, it is possible. Does it come easy? No, but what it becomes is a starting place.

Even though during the past two decades single parenting has become an acceptable practice and the role of men being more active in the role of a father is changing, it still does not erase nor invalidate the hole in the soul. God did not intend for broken marriages and out-of-wedlock births to become common practice. In order to prove that we as women especially can have our independence and do our own thing, we have deprived our children of what is their godly, inherited right as a son or daughter – the impartation and impact a father brings to their upbringing.

My parenting skills, like those of my parents, have been based off of the previous generations' ability to raise their children, not to mention if the mothers were sensitive and supportive or firm and mean. I was involved in a few teen pregnancy studies during my undergraduate and graduate degree work and believe once a teenager becomes pregnant, her mental functions cease to grow for the moment because her whole focus, whether she will admit it or not, is on the life she is carrying. She becomes unstable, depressed and many are moved to the point of not finishing school. Being involved with these studies and working with the pregnant teens and listening to their stories has made me a firm believer that the reverse occurs when the father is present and the daughter has a relationship with him. She becomes a reflection of stability and possesses the potential to finish school (not pregnant), not end up in jail, on drugs, involved with gangs or depressed.

With the normal growth and development of our lives disrupted, we develop a hunger for what our fathers did not impart into us – we develop a longing for *daddy*, which we try to suppress, but the sad part is that this longing continues to haunt us, even into our adulthood. As we have children, repeating the pattern of our parents, we impart this same longing in them. It was evident my son longed for his father, even though I tried to fill that emptiness in his life. We end up spending a lifetime searching, trying to feel the void – the hole in our souls.

My freedom from the longing, the hole, began once I was able to acknowledge and understand my father's absence in my life. The freer I became, the more I recognized and pursued my rightful inheritance in God, no longer a bastard. I had to forgive my father. My spiritual father and pastor, Dr. Stephen Rathod, did a study on forgiveness and in it he stated, *"When you forgive you are loosening yourself from those you are tied to,"* meaning that you are freeing yourself from the emotional ties, emotional bondage that once so easily made you unbalanced. In other words, cut the strings and set yourself free.

A few years after my mother died, my sisters were sitting around saying what we wished my mother had said and had done. While we were talking, I heard *how could you hold your mother accountable for what she did not know?* She did the best she could with what she had. Later I shared this with my sisters and we all sat around shocked once we realized the impact of the words, and began looking at the things we were doing as parents as well. I had to do the same with my father. I could not hold him accountable for what he did not know. His parents did not raise him to be a father, but a son and that was all he knew.

It became a necessity for my survival that I forgive my father for the damage, the void, the hole, the hurt, the rejection, the abandonment, and the denial that had been inflicted upon my soul by him not being there. I had to make peace with myself, and then forgive myself for continuing with this unhealthy pattern in my life. It had come to the point that I had let those issues rule me. I had let my bastard status, brought on by my parents, make the decisions for my life. You know the questions we ask: *What will people say? How will they treat me?* Etc., etc., etc. I had let these unanswered questions control my life. I have now chosen to move on.

Once you forgive someone, doubt will come into your mind and make you question if you have truly forgiven that person, but know this, that if you were sincere in your approach, then truly you have forgiven that person. At this point you ask God to help heal you, for you cannot do it alone. I had to do this with my father because his abandonment and rejection of me cut deep, and I was not even aware of the magnification until I went to stay with him for a short period of time. My disappointment in staying with him was that I wanted to develop a relationship with him and he did not. What I guess is even sadder is that those around me even suggested I quit trying to because if he did not want a relationship with them, he surely would not want one with me. I later understood it was not that he did not want a relationship with his family; it was that he did not know how to have a relationship or be in one.

Without forgiveness, there can be no inner healing. After releasing the hurt, I had to let God heal my wounds. He poured the healing balm of Gilead over me for my healing process to begin. Am I totally whole right now? Not yet, but I am on my way there. I know I cannot just cover up my hurt because it will scab over. What will happen is I will still not be healed. The scab will serve as a constant reminder of what my father did not do for me. This is not how I wish to live my life anymore. Whenever my spiritual father and pastor prayed for me he would say, *"Father God, let her come to know the love of a father."* For a whole year he prayed that over me.

Total forgiveness does not mean reconciliation. It does not mean that once it is said and done you will come together as if nothing has happened. Total forgiveness is when you can release those who have hurt you, wounded you; you can forgive them, pray for them, and finally bless them. Forgiveness will destroy the dividing line between a father and daughter, between a father and son and the past memories of the wrong or perceived wrongs done by each. I encourage you to get the blame out of your system! Yell about it! Rant about it! Tell someone who you trust about it! Get the guilt and hurt out of your system. Then once you are finished, step back and let the Holy Spirit work in you, tell Him, *"Now, Father God, I am ready to let go and forgive!"*

Chapter 10
❧ A New Vision of Fatherhood ❧

*"The ultimate measure of a man
is not where he stands in moments
of comfort and convenience,
but where he stands at times of
challenge and controversy."*
- Anonymous

A new vision of fatherhood has the potential to rise in the circle of parenting. Men can be effective, with a secure place in the family and be the father God created them to be. However, the power to truly be an effective father will come alive during the small moments in which one spends with his son, his daughter, or his family. Do not become the shadow seen or reflected in pictures, videos, etc., but chose to become active, rather than remaining passive. Be eager and willing to fulfill the journey of fatherhood. The new vision of fatherhood must be laced with love, a love that is pure, sincere and genuine – a love that does not demand that your son or daughter meet your expectations, but a love that will help exceed them.

Going back to before post-industrial times, a father's role was defined. They were to provide, be responsible for their children's moral, spiritual and educational upbringing. They introduced their children to work ethics, social life, etc. The post-industrial era brought struggles that created havoc. Women have biological clocks; men have financial clocks. As parents men and women try to balance work, home, children, marriage, relationships and community. The times have brought with it increased rates of teen suicides, pregnancy, poverty and plummeting test scores, just to name a few.

Fatherhood is a blessing, a gift and a reward. Men and women both must change their perspectives of fatherhood and be willing to make changes that have a positive impact on families. I invite all men to share in a dimension of fatherhood that goes beyond standard definitions. I feel like fathers are becoming hungry for more than being the provider, disciplinarian, etc. They want to become involved in creating a better life for their children.

By building a spiritual life for your children, you, as a father, begin to fulfill your life. The journey toward adulthood, being whole, being full, begins. This will, I believe, reverse the movement of fatherlessness. It will end the cultural silence that engulfs fatherhood. It will attempt to replace guilt, blame, shame and neglect with beauty, reward, depth and fulfillment. Take the hand of a father and guide your children. Make them your choice. Make a choice to be a real man, a father. Fathers, you have the power and potential to influence your children. They are waiting and listening for your words of encouragement, for your actions, for you. Do not let your love for them be lost, then found too late.

Choose to become deeply rooted in your child's life; stop being a nomad, a wanderer. Good, godly men carry masculine traits while at the same time, revealing new ones – nurturing, emotionally sensitive, etc. Contrary to popular belief – fathers are not expendable.

Your job is to keep your child's spirit, hope and love alive. You are very important to the development of your children. Strengthen your faithfulness to the task of fathering. Fathering is not easy; there is no straightforward man-made baby book on fatherhood.

If you are a man who chooses not to have children and be a father, that is your choice. However, if you are a man who is a father and you feel fathering is unnatural or uncomfortable, search yourself and ask what demons you need to confront to set yourself free. You cannot set yourself free with your money, your job, your prestige, your height, or your weight (and you cannot impress or convince your children either).

Be examples of how to develop a sense of balance in one's life without feeling guilty. I encourage men to stop viewing fathers only as a "provider," the "breadwinner." This is not your sole responsibility in the lives of your children. You are more than that. Do not disengage from your child's life; be active, no longer passive.

Fathers, if you want to damage a relationship – hide. This will surely damage your relationships. Stop disappearing, stop the vanishing act, and stop hiding from your wife, your children, yourself. Stop working to please the demons of your past. Also, get out from the box society has built for you and your role as husband and father. Make a choice to not become the stereotypical father of generations past, emotionally distant.

To every father and every potential father, I say:

Be involved with your children, nurture them, and spend time with them (quality is better than quantity, when dictated or warranted). Be an influence in your children, help them believe in themselves, help them to know they are a person of value, of worth. The end result is your life will be richer for it; and as you nurture your children, focus on nurturing your relationship with your wife as well.

Remember fatherhood is not a chore but a journey filled with adventure, drama, chaos, etc.

And women, mothers for those fathers trying to be a part of their child's life, stop fighting them. Stop being an obstruction to your child's development. Believe or not, women are territorial creatures, so let us say to our fathers "It is okay to come in and participate." Fathers, we need your insight, your partnership and leadership. Know that while you are shaping your children, you are shaping their present as well as their future.

When life goes in slow motion, take advantage of it, for then you will be able to clearly see some things you may not have paid attention to before. Direct your energy toward rebuilding your families, your communities. I want to encourage you to search and find your place in fatherhood; no longer continue to let society define your dreams, your ideas, your plans, your desire to be the best father you can be. Find meaning in relationships, actions and values – treasure your wife, your children and your time with them.

The healing of wounds left by our fathers is a process, and a long one at that. One part of the healing process is grieving — grieving what you have lost, what you needed, what you wanted.

Whether you are in midlife, teen or senior, you must mourn, you must cry, you must realize there are some things you may never get from your fathers. It requires us to confront how deep our own neediness runs and when we do, we are able to see our fathers had the same issues.

Through this we are able to gain understanding of our fathers and then are able to forgive them. I encourage you fathers not to let fear, hatred, bitterness or disinterest keep you in bondage.

To develop a richer, fuller sense of self, our inner image of our fathers must be healed. It will require us to untangle, unweave the fantasies, the myths, the hopes and the wishes. It means seizing the opportunity to change by pulling up our past, looking at our present and choosing to build a better foundation for our future. Now is the time to throw out the fragmented father images and chose a strong, godly father.

Time is moving. Make a choice for the better. Life is tough and getting tougher. Choose to be there for your children. Even if you don't have all the answers, even if you can't calm all of their fears, choose to be there. Choose to be responsible, choose to become the father you want your children to have, that you want to be and that you want them to remember, because theirs is the image of a father that will be instilled in their spirits, their hearts and their memories. Instilling roots in your children gives them a sense of strength and identity.

Once you confront it, let go of the insanity of your past, for now is the dawning of a new day, the end of a generational destructive cycle and the beginning of a new foundation. Now is the time to look ahead with confidence, no longer looking back with regrets. The challenge of the new vision of fatherhood is:

- Change in our attitudes about fatherhood;
- Change in our family value systems;
- Communicate, effectively and openly;
- Be involved;
- Develop a sense of responsibility;
- Acknowledge the worth of fatherhood;
- Honor, work and worth but not at the expense of your family, your children;
- Fight negative stereotypes;
- Fight governmental/company policies that are rigid in their view of fathers and families.

Fatherhood should be valued for then it can create some magical moments in our lives, our children's lives and the generations to come.

Chapter 11
❧ The Blessings of A Father ❧

*"A man cannot leave a
better legacy to the world
than a well-educated family."*
~ Thomas Scott

Every child longs for a father like in the fairy tales. He is there and returns even when he goes off on quests. He is not perfect but he stays around, married to the same woman. He is the man of the family and would never substitute anything for his family because he values their importance.

What becomes important to us is that he is there – the man of the home who is not only our biological father, but spiritual one as well. He is the one who helps form our identity. Words like divorce, adultery, child support, paternity suits, custody battles, blended families are not a part of his vocabulary. He does not use these words in the same sentence with his family. As a father, he becomes a structured embodiment of biblical and moral principles and one who believes in fatherhood, its necessity and wholeness. This breed of man is rare and hard to find. Every child longs for the blessings of a father.

In Psalm 128 (paraphrased): *"The father when he is sturdy and godly becomes a solid wall for his family and the mother in turn becomes the vine, which grows up the wall and the result of the efforts of both produces fruitfulness. It produces a legacy that lives on for hundreds of years."* An essential basis for our foundation is that the father is there for you; this becomes the legacy to be left behind. God built in us an innate desire to emulate or imitate our fathers, who imitate Him. God never sends out mixed messages, so why do our fathers send them out? I would like to believe they do so without cruel intentions, without understanding this hinders our growth to become self-sufficient in our adult lives.

One of the blessings the father imparts is by giving us a male perspective on life. This is an important phase of background in our life; without it we are forced to move on with an unfinished stage. By being involved in our lives, a father produces a profound impact setting the stage for the development of our being whole, well-rounded. It is a blessing and responsibility of the father to shape his child's behavior, to develop an emotional connection to his child.

Another blessing from a father can be found in Dr. Myles Munroe's book, *The Principle of Fatherhood: Priority, Position and the Role of the Male*. Dr. Munroe says " . . . *that fathers must develop fathers and understand that (God's) children are always becoming. . . . A successful father will produce a child who is greater than himself."* Dr. Munroe goes further to say that if you are satisfied with your child being only as good as you, then *you have failed your child as a father.*

John Maxwell once said, *"A dream together with a positive attitude produces a person with unlimited possibilities and potential."* I would like to take that a step further to include family. Once a father hears the dream of his child, it is by his encouragement that she will begin to pursue the dream, giving her a positive attitude that he bestows on her – this is the blessings of a father, which produces a child with unlimited potential.

A father's involvement by interaction, availability and responsibility adds to him blessing his children. According to a study done by M. E. Lamb, a father can interact with his child through caregiving and sharing in the child's activities. A father's *availability* is done by being present or available to his child; and a father's *responsibility* is taking care of his child, making arrangement for the child's provision.

In return, the father gets to see his children imitate him, his characteristics of confidence, courage, success, leadership and skill. He gets to see the payoff of his involvement – a child who has been created *whole in her soul* – emotional, social, physical, spiritual and intellectual. The father knows he has helped raise a child who is self confident, willing and has a greater tolerance for stress and frustration.

Fathers who, by choice or chance, are **not** involved in the lives of the children they help produce miss out on a valuable experience and a satisfying relationship. This is an experience that is irreplaceable. I love my relationship with my son. We can talk about anything and I do mean anything. He knows there is nothing he cannot say to me or tell me. For those of you who were raised without the presence of your father, know this: if no one else appreciates you, God not only appreciates you, but He values your uniqueness.

When I arrived at Covenant Family Church, I did not know what to expect. I had heard of the pastor and his anointing for being *father-like*, but it still made me apprehensive. Why? I did not know what to expect of a father. I did not know what to look for. My plan was to go to church and wait out my sentence. I did not want to get involved because I was pretty sure God was not going to use me any more. The pastor's abruptness signaled to me impatience and sent a blow to my already shattered, unsteady sense of self-worth. This was a sure sign God was going to send me somewhere else so I could be left alone to lick my wounds. I believed God was going to provide me with a church to run to, where I could find grace and mercy.

Why do we do this? Why do we run when we get hurt? I believe so often it is because we want the television dads and not the real life ones. This is not a game, so why are we playing? Our self -worth and value are at stake. Running from church to church or bed to bed will not fill the hole left inside. It will not even begin to heal, but becoming runny and pus-like with infection. Stop the running and deal with the issue.

In a woman's life, her father can empower her, give her the authority to pursue without feeling guilty and ashamed. The word *authority* in Greek actually means, *"to stand forth with power and dignity."* I did not realize the authority I had until my back was up against a wall; preparing to write this book tested my determination. I love it when people comment to me that I am a strong woman like my mother. My mother was my first and lasting impression of authority. She put in me the best she could of what my father should have done. Now, after being under my spiritual father, Dr. Stephen Rathod, I consider it an honor to be called daughter by him, but more so, I am bestowed with the privilege to be called daughter of the Most High God.

I have the authority to stand firm with power and dignity. From within, I have learned I am the author of my own identity and God is the One who authorized me. I had to learn to build a solid foundation and find my own ground to stand on, my own authority. He has given me the gumption to act on my own behalf for my vision, my soul and my purpose. I can be gentle, fierce, waiting, leaping and yet always knowing who I am in Christ. By giving myself to my purpose, I have developed a quality of belonging to myself and to God.

My father is not perfect, and for that matter, none of them is. By recognizing the cause for the hole in my soul, the one left by him and by forgiving him, I am able to begin to build a solid, sure foundation. I am finally able to live peaceably with myself, knowing my life has value and worth. I wanted to change for the better and I have. I also had to recognize God did not put me in this world to judge my parents, or even to make sure they learned their lessons, which is His job. My job was to become more conscious of my lessons, my responsibilities and to learn from the classroom of life that God has placed me in. I am responsible for my thinking and my choices. I am responsible for loving me. Fanny Fern once said, *"To me the name of father was another name for love."* My goal is to strive so when I hear the word *father* I can associate it with the word *love* and *not feelings of insignificance*. When we hear the name father, we feel love, we know love and that love embraces us unashamedly.

Chapter 12
❧ A Woman Bared ❧

"Your vision will become clear only
when you look into your heart . . .
who looks outside, dreams,
who looks inside, awakens."
~ Carl Jung

I begin this chapter as a woman bare. Carl Jung is truly correct in his point of view with this quote. Once I began to look inside myself, I started to wake up. I have allowed God to begin to strip away things I have let hinder me – the excess baggage of my past, my feelings and emotions of the past that have clouded my future, my destiny and my divine mandate. Due to the void from not having my father raise me, I found I tend to make so-called safe choices, avoiding those that are artistic and risky endeavors, even though my heart inclines that way, even though these are the choices I desire. Here is the bottom line – unless you face it and say I have a problem, even God cannot help you.

Once I came to terms with what was going on in my life, I began to seek God and found I have learned and lived during my journey by looking closely at my relationship with my father. I can begin to affect my world now in the most intimate, natural and reflective ways. Determined to change my life, I no longer see myself trying a hundred different ways to please other people. Though, I have yet to say good-bye to the little child within, I am learning to celebrate myself once again.

There are times I have often wondered if my father thought that not being part of my life was a terrible loss. My father's lack of impartation affected my economic status, my religious practice, my educational background and my individualism. I would like to think my father wanted more of a role in my life than being limited to conception. Even though my father had little contact with me, I would like to believe he wanted to work and provide for me. My heart wants to believe my father does not consider or look at our relationship as being marked by shame, resentment and detachment, the same abandonment and rejection I suffered from. I would like to believe in his heart, my father secretly yearns to succeed at being a father.

Fathering is unique, just as being a man is unique. You will find no two alike even if they are identical twins. I have come to view fatherhood by seeing past the imbalances and desiring to see a change, one of a major influence in a child's life instead of an ineffective role model. Any father's bond with his child is in need of nurturing. It will involve rediscovering each other, confronting the past, present and the future, while strengthening their relationship and bond. As one who has come through the bastard status, I would like to not see society continue to dictate a father's involvement in his child's life. I desire for the father to become involved in our lives, regardless of how old we are. It is never too late.

Fathers, you have another option – an option to get to know us, to impart into us, to love us, to bless us. Whether you realize it or not, absent or present, you play a critical role in shaping our attitudes, our aspirations and our dreams, especially in the life of a daughter. It is interesting that a father can cause us to aim high far more than a mother can.

Marriage is the pathway to effective fatherhood. We need to learn to do relationships like godly marriages. Write things down and weigh the good versus the bad

– purposing that even if the bad outweighs the good, the relationship is worth restoring. What my father did not do far outweighed what he did do. I am not taking lightly what my father **has** done. My prayer is that the role of a father becomes a positive, ongoing one in the lives of the children he brings into the world.

Life is like an echo. Whatever we send out comes back to us. If we constantly confess we are bastards because we had no fathers, this will come back to us only to compound our present situation. However, if we begin to echo even though my father was not there, I am more than a conqueror, so shall we be.

I had to learn to love me. It has been said *intimacy is like an immune system for one's soul.* When you learn to love yourself, you are able to battle the psychological infections of abandonment, rejection, discouragement, inadequacy, insignificance, insecurity and loss of worth. When you love yourself you begin to feel accepted, confident, empowered to endure. By being in love with yourself, you are fair to yourself, giving yourself both quantity and quality time. You are authorized to be and achieve, because you love and believe in you! When you lie, cheat and steal from yourself, you have deprived yourself of what can be truly yours.

In Numbers 14:6-9 it says:

6) And Joshua the son of Nun, and Caleb the son Jephunneh, which were of them that searched the land, rent their clothes;

7) And they spake unto all the company of the children of Israel, saying the land, which we passed through to search it, is an exceeding good land.

8) If the LORD delight in us, then he will bring us into this land, and give it us; a land which floweth with milk and honey.

9) Only rebel not ye against the LORD, neither fear ye the people of the land; for they are bread for us: their defence is departed from them, and the LORD is with us: fear them not.

Even though society has labeled you and me bastards because of being born out of wedlock, God says otherwise. Like Caleb and Joshua, we are well able to take the land and it is rightfully ours. Jesus redeemed us from the bastard status. Unless the love we seek is built on Christ, we will not get the love we crave or desire. We will not be content or satisfied, which means we will continue to look for ourselves.

I spent all these years trying to find me
Through others, classes, churches,
committees, communities, conferences.
I have traveled here and there and back again
Still trying to find me.
More classes, books, talks, discussions,
But I am no where to be found
I spent all these years trying to find me
Could it be,
I wasn't lost after all.

© *Java L. Collins 2006*

As you look back at your past, you will detect the true source of your hole. The hole in your soul becomes larger when you continue to pull around the excess baggage. Until you make a decision to confront it, deal with it, cut it loose, forgive, heal and move on, the hole will continue to be a part of your life.

I want to leave you with five promises to yourself:

1. Encourage yourself to be proud of who you are;
2. Love yourself;
3. Keep your body, soul and spirit healthy.
4. Let all parts of your life be characterized with integrity.
5. Treat all people honestly.

God is a loving Father and He loves me just as I am. He is teaching and grooming me in how to be a daughter. He had to teach me to stop struggling with myself and renew, strengthen myself, so I could sing again. I had to learn my father's sins are his own, and no longer mine because of the blood of Jesus; it is settled. God has instilled in me the power to prevail and He celebrates with me when I do. He taught me that in spite of my fatherless or perverted father state, He has brought me through childhood and adolescence to womanhood and with power. I have learned that when I go beyond the boundaries that God has set for me, I give more weight to the opinion of others than to God. *My choice is to no longer give others control of my life.*

On Father's Day, I received my emancipation from the curses that had hounded my life about being a bastard.

I believe with all my heart the curses have been broken – I am no longer guilty because of what was done by my parents and that God is on my side. My life is no longer based on what man says about me or to me, but what God has said. He has made me and called me. I am a chosen vessel, a treasure.

My heart is that I believe by sharing with you I am letting you know what is possible. I am saying that within the deepest part of you lies your true self and it is a thing of beauty and power. It is to be embraced, loved and celebrated regardless of whether your natural father was there or not.   It is a choice which only you can make. I believe your spirit, your heart, can be a seed. Go, choose where you want to plant it! Do not let the bastard status or fatherless status continue to hold you hostage one day longer. Go plant your seed!

As I live each day I no longer pretend I am okay when I am not, but I have determined not to be *emotionally raped* anymore by choosing to live life to its fullest measure, which is hard because I had never been taught how or shown the way. I had to learn my issues – my hole –was something for me to deal with, but I had to realize my hole does not define who I am. So, I say to you do not let your *hole*, what you have not received, define who you are and keep you from being *whole*.

Scars from the absence of a father can be healed with time, forgiveness and love. The life I now live is a miracle by the grace of God. I had come into a relationship with God with my heart broken, my strength failed, my purpose crippled and my dreams shattered. There are times I feel like a princess on top of the world and there are times I feel like laughter has been denied in my life. I have stopped looking for the happily ever after ending, for the best I hope for now is to find hope, love and inspiration with those I love and who love me, realizing God is the only one who can fill the hole, not man. I have learned to tell myself I love you and appreciate all you do. The toughest lesson I have learned through this whole process is that *I do not have to please anyone in order to be loved*. If someone cannot accept me for who I am, then that is their loss, for they have missed the chance to make a great friend for life.

The Beauty of Ugliness

"I am the rose of Sharon, And the lily of the valleys.
As a lily among thorns, so is my love among the daughters."
- Song of Solomon 2:1-2

I see a lily surrounded by thorns.
At a glance,
It looks like it will be threatened
By the very existence of the thorns,
Surrounding the beauty of the lily.

Why are the thorns there?
I ask.
He looks at me and smiles.

Well, they are situations,
Circumstances,
And things
Which have tried to hinder the beauty of the lily.
They're abuse,
Neglect,
Isolation,
Abandonment,
Rejection,
Being unloved,
Deception,
But most of all,
Misperception, to name a few.

They're the hurt,
The pain,
The tears,
The fears,
The cries in the night,
And some done even in the light.

They represent the past,
The present,
And fear of the future.
They are things, which set out to destroy
The beauty of the lily.

I leaned closer to the lily,
Because a glimmer of something caught my eye.
And as I peered,
I saw an almost invisible layer glittering,
Resembling that of a bubble being blown.
There were colors arrayed,
Surrounding the lily in splendor.
The awe of its beauty
Took my breath away.

What's that? I asked,
As I looked with longing eyes.
That's Me, says the Father.
Protecting the love that the lily holds within,
Keeping out what shouldn't be,
Until time for Me to come in,
And reveal the beauty of the lily in its fullness.
I protect what's Mine until the very end.

Wow, I said softly,
I wish that could be me.
As He smiled,
Tears appeared in His eyes,
He gently took my face in His hands and said,
"My daughter, it's been you all this time."

©*Java L. Collins 1998*

References/Suggested Readings

The Holy Bible. (1982). New King James Version. Nashville, TN: Thomas Nelson Publishers.

Abbott, John S.C., Rev. (1842). *The Mother at Home: or The Principles of Maternal Duty.* NY: American Tract Society.

Appleton, William S. Dr. (1987). *Fathers and Daughters.* CA: Berkley Press.

Blankenhorn, David. (1995). *Fatherless America: Confronting Our Most Urgent Social Problem.* London, England: Harper Perennial.

Bozett, Frederick W. and Hanson, Shirley M. H. (eds.) (1991). *Fatherhood and Families in Cultural Context.* NY: Springer Publishing Company.

Henry, Dewitt (ed.) and McPherson, James Allen (ed.). (1998). *Fathering Daughters: Reflections by Men.* MA: Beacon Press.

Lamb, M. E. (ed.). (1987). *The Role of the Father in Child Development.* 3rd Ed., pp 66-103. NY: Wiley Publishers.

Marone, Nicky. (1992). *How to Father a Successful Daughter.* NY: Ballentine Books.

Munroe, Myles. (2001). *The Principle of Fatherhood.* Lanham, MD: Pneuma Life Publishing.

Acknowledgments

There are so many to thank who have been in my corner and believed in me, when I struggled to believe in myself. With God as my mainstay, those involved reminded me of His love for me and His desire to use me as a vessel for writing. To my son, Milton, thank you for your artistic and creative eye when viewing the covers. To my sisters, Demetria and Dorothy, and my friends, Grace and Louise, thank you for your watchful eyes and comments while reviewing this manuscript, as well as your much needed prayers.

To Marcia Freespirit and the JimSam Inc. Publishing, thank you so much for your diligence, caring and partnering with me to pursue my dream. And to Michele Ash, I consider you to be not only a top notch editor but a welcomed new friend. As always, a special thanks to my spiritual father and pastor, Dr. Stephen Rathod; thank you for loving me, guiding me and being there for me. To many countless others, thank you for encouraging me.

Praise for *A Letter To My Sisters: An Awakening of Dreams*

"Ms. Collins talked about the things she went through and how she overcame them. The determination to accomplish what is in her heart and her vision and the boldness to do it is to be admired . . . I am sure it [this book] will give strength to those who read it that they, too, can accomplish all that God has put in their hearts through faith and trust in God."

Lee Rathod
First Lady, Covenant Family Church
Tulsa, OK

"Insightful, delightful; with wisdom beyond her years, Collins challenges all women to live each and every day to its fullest. Through this work and scripture, Collins gently guides her "sisters" to the understanding that there is a time for embracing oneself."

Priscilla Dougherty
VP, Treasury Services - Mgmt
Bank of Oklahoma
Tulsa, OK

"Wow! From the time I opened this book I couldn't put it down. It was like the author wrote this book just for me. Like she was speaking to my heart. It was so good that I bought a copy of this book for every woman in my family. Thank you so much, Java L. Collins, for writing this book."

O. M. White-David
Las Vegas, NV

"Ms. Collins' book was wonderful. I read the whole book in one morning and couldn't put it down until I was finished with it. I am so ready to read the next one."

Deloris Thomas
Oklahoma City, OK

If you ever want to read a book that is without a doubt inspired by God's divine revelation and not just another book, then read *A Letter To My Sisters*. I am not saying this just because the author has stuck by me through thick and thin and has been an incredibly real sister to me, but this book made me laugh, cry and feel so close, so intimate with God. This book is so down-to- earth, so amazingly practical, you're going to feel like you know her. You will find strength after reading about her road from brokenness to recovery.

Sonja Henderson
Covenant Family Church
Tulsa, OK

"I recently read Java Collin's book, *To My Sisters*. It was a very appropriate book at a very appropriate time in my life. Although I have two sisters by blood, I have three extremely close friends who are sisters of my heart. One of my "sisters" recently lost her husband to suicide, was diagnosed with cancer and was battling anorexia as well. As friends and sisters do, the three healthy "sisters" rallied to support the other sister during this extremely difficult time. We were all hurting from the loss of the husband, and then scared of losing our beloved one to cancer. We were shaken to the core. I purchased this book for each of us. The book helped to strengthen us and give us the courage and insight to remember what is important and what is not. We have all been changed by the events of the past eighteen months, but Java's book truly inspired us to look within. It's like Java was speaking to us on many different levels. We will all be thankful and better women as a result of reading this book. Whether someone is facing difficult times or not, this is a must read book for women of all walks of life and it all situations."

Jan Tyler, VP
Sr. Product Manager, Treasury Services
BOK Financial
Tulsa, OK

Excerpts from the author's other books

My Journey: The Beauty of the Valley

My Journey: The Beauty of the Valley: a four-part collection of poetic and prophetic psalms. So often we get tied up physically, emotionally and spiritually when things aren't going our way, and these distractions create an imbalance in us, leaving in its quake a wondering about who we are, why me, etc.

My Journey begins to deal more with worshipping God, regardless of where you are in life, regardless of the situations and circumstances. It puts into practice speaking the word, in season and out, to bring us hope, life and love. This book reflects upon the complexity of emotions we feel, but more so it directs how we feel toward God. It brings us to an awakening in ourselves of who God is and trying to see Him as Father, while making the journey toward spiritual transformation, self – discovery and finding fulfillment in God and His Word. He gives us the reassurance that He has been there all the time.

ISBN 1-882185-60-9 - *My Journey: The Beauty of the Valley,* Cornerstone Publishing
Available at these websites: CornerstonePublishing.com, Amazon.com, Barnes and Noble, Target.com

A Letter to My Sisters: An Awakening of Dreams!
> *When you dare to pursue your dreams, my Sisters, you must prepare yourself for change in the process. You must be prepared to enter a time of transition, where nothing will seem stable. Where you will speak and cry out to the Lord, yet hear nothing but stillness.*

A Letter to My Sisters: An Awakening of Dreams! Offers an autobiographical work in which the author shares a journal of her reflections of her journey to dream again and examines her thoughts on the guidance received from her faith. It is a journey toward fulfillment and self-discovery. It is a "must read" for every woman yearning to make a step toward wholeness!

ISBN-10: 1882185617, ISBN-13: 978-1882185610 – *A Letter to My Sisters: An Awakening of Dreams!* Cornerstone Publishing

About the Author
Writing to make a difference!

Java L. Collins, MHR, is a vibrant woman of God, born in Coffeyville, Kansas and raised in Tulsa, Oklahoma. She is a gifted and talented author, speaker and educator, who holds degrees in education, liberal arts, psychology and human relations. In searching for the answers to life's numerous questions and challenges, Ms. Collins became a *"God chaser"* before realizing God was unveiling her true destiny.

Ms. Collins' goal is to use all she has learned in her professional, educational and personal life experiences to teach, counsel and empower others – especially women – to a more fulfilling and godly lifestyle with healing of relationships with self and others. Her passion and life focus is on teaching and training, not only for this generation, but the next generation as well according to Psalm 145:4 – *One generation will commend your works to another.* She has developed an understanding of brokenness, a heart for healing and restoring through the power of God, which is necessary to reach wholeness. She believes *"You are a whole person going somewhere and about to accomplish something."*

A professor once said, *"Words can be teachers."* Ms. Collins believes writing heals, brings harmony, helps one to discover one's voice, ministers to the spirit, gives us hope, makes us cry, speaks to our souls. Writing will show the contents of one's heart through glorious words and hard truths. Thoughts are challenged, hearts touched and a teachable encounter with God occurs when allowed. Writing produces words with the power to soften or harden, inform or confuse, clarify or cloud. Written words have the power to produce change.

Ms. Collins knows she has been called by God to *set the captives free* with her writings, but she also knows the reality that *as the heart cries, it speaks* – but who is willing to listen to its aches and tears to find answers? It is the desire of her heart that these writings minister to all who read them, setting free the dream within.

Ms. Collins currently resides in Tulsa, Oklahoma and is a member of Covenant Family Church. You may contact Ms. Collins at javasheartcry@yahoo.com.

Romans 12:11-13

Never be lacking in zeal,
but keep your spiritual fervor,
serving the Lord.
Be joyful in hope, patient in affliction, faithful in prayer.
Share with God's people who are in need. (NIV)

Please visit our website at
www.JimSamInc.com
to order additional copies.

JimSam Inc. Publishing
P.O. Box 3363
Riverview, FL 33568
813.748.9523

Lightning Source Inc.
LaVergne, TN USA
14 August 2009

154858LV00002B/3/P